METALWORKING
TOOLS AND TECHNIQUES

METALWORKING
TOOLS AND TECHNIQUES

STAN BRAY

The Crowood Press

First published in 2003 by
The Crowood Press Ltd
Ramsbury, Marlborough
Wiltshire SN8 2HR

www.crowood.com

British Library Cataloguing-in-Publication Data
A catalogue record for this book is available from the British Library.

ISBN 1 86126 573 5

All photographs and line drawings by the author.

Frontispiece The governor on a model steam engine. Although it appears to
be of simple construction, making it requires nearly every form of discipline
described in this book.

Disclaimer
Safety is of the utmost importance in every aspect of metalworking.
When using tools, always follow closely the manufacturer's recommended
procedures. However, the author and publisher cannot accept responsibility for
any accident or injury caused by following the advice given in this book.

Designed and typeset by Focus Publishing,
11a St Botolph's Road, Sevenoaks, Kent TN13 2AJ

Printed and bound in Malaysia by Times Offset (M) Sdn. Bhd.

Contents

Introduction

Metalworking as both a profession and a means of relaxation started with the Bronze Age, when the human race first realized the value of using metal. We do not know, of course, exactly who first discovered that metal could be made by using natural materials found in the ground, and that tools made from metal were superior to those hewn from wood and stone, but it is of interest that techniques used by those primitive people form the basis of some methods that are still used to make metal. These techniques have naturally been refined and improved, but the basics are still there – ore is heated to form the metal, which is then shaped one way or another into tools that will in themselves be used to fabricate other items from metal. While primitive humans had to make their own or borrow other people's tools with which to work, we are now in the fortunate position of being able, if we wish, to purchase most of the items we need. However, in some facets of metal-working it is still necessary to make certain tools for oneself, and also many people find satisfaction in having created the implement with which they will do a job.

This book is intended to offer guidance to anyone interested in metalworking, be they budding engineers or hobbyists. For the newcomer to the subject, there is advice on how to make a start and how to progress once having made that start. While modern materials and machinery have changed so much that a craftsman of even fifty years ago would not recognize them, a number of the techniques used have remained unchanged for hundreds of years. In addition to offering help to the beginner, the reader will find some information on more advanced work and in particular the use of modern materials and methods as far as they are likely to be needed in a small workshop.

As a hobby, metalworking covers a very wide range of interests, such as making jewellery, horology, motor vehicle repairs, fancy ironwork for home decoration and model-making. Some aspects of the work are common to all metal-working. Some skills will only be pertinent to one particular type of work, although it is still necessary to be conversant with the basics that are common to all types. For example, no matter what one's interests, it will still be necessary to be able to saw and file accurately, read drawings and drill a hole in the right place. When we come to lathe work the methods described will be suitable for any aspect of metalworking, and in general the only difference between the work done by a clock-maker and that of someone wishing to restore an army tank will be in the size of the machinery and tools, as well as the metal used.

People from all walks of life use metal-working as a means of relaxation and it is something that exercises the mind, because no matter how much one learns there is always something new to be discovered. Time spent can be very rewarding, not only as far as the end product is concerned, but also in the relaxation and therapeutic effect to be derived from the process. It is to be hoped that this book will offer encouragement and help to all who are interested in metalworking, and perhaps create an interest to those seeking a worthwhile hobby.

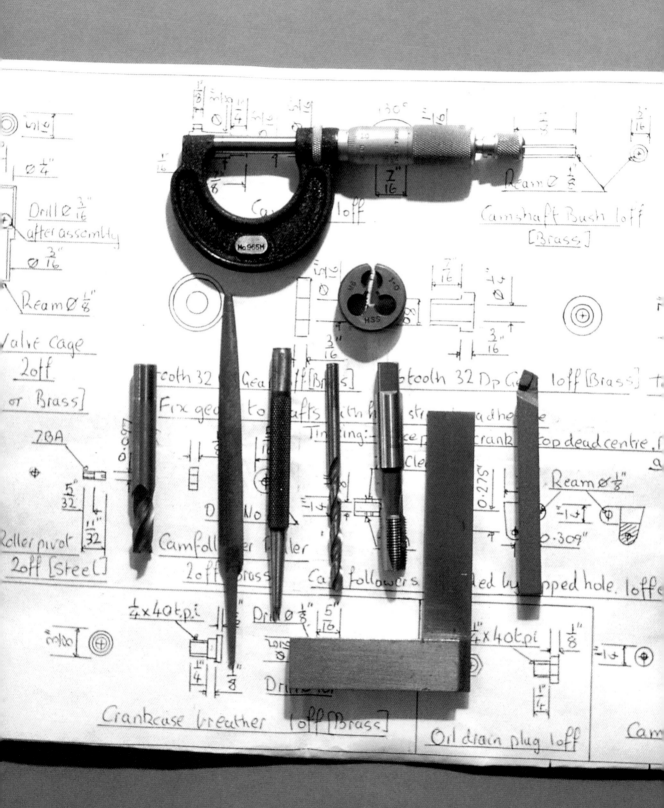

1 The Working Environment

When setting up a workshop for the metal-worker, there are a number of things that must be considered. It needs to have sufficient room in which to house any machinery that may be required, plenty of light and heat, and while some people will be happy using quite basic facilities, others will want to install additional comforts such as a seat, radio and sometimes even facilities for making light refreshments. How useful and efficient the workshop ultimately becomes as a place in which to work and relax will be in the hands of the individual; continual improvements will inevitably be made in order to make the best of whatever building is available to use.

SAFETY

In General

It is essential that, right from the start, considerable thought is given to safety. Not only should we consider the owner of the workshop, but also anybody who may decide to pay a visit, especially as people with no experience of a workshop environment are likely to want to see what goes on. When installing benches, equipment, shelving and so on, make sure that there are no protrusions on which people can hurt themselves or damage their clothing. Ensure that there are no loose electrical wires or odd tools left lying on the floor to be tripped over. If liquids are spilled on the floor, they must be immediately cleaned up so that it is not possible to slip on them.

Benches and machinery should be installed in positions that allow for evacuation should a fire occur. It may also be worth considering whether or not any window would be available as an emergency means of escape. Keep a fire extinguisher or fire blanket, or both, readily available. Make sure that all electrical wiring is maintained in good condition.

It is wise to take precautions against fire. Under no circumstances should water be used to quench a fire in the workshop. Keep an extinguisher or a fire blanket such as this readily available.

Safety Practices

Some simple safety precautions should also be observed when working, for example *never* leave chuck keys in their chucks when the chucks are fitted to a machine. If forgotten and the machine is started up, the chuck key will fly out across the workshop, possibly hitting somebody and causing a nasty injury, or at the very least it will cause some damage. Loose sleeves can result in nasty injuries as they are liable to catch in revolving machinery; an elastic band round the wrist will prevent this from happening. Have some means of communication with you when working – a mobile telephone or a simple intercom system such as baby alarm will enable help to be summoned if needed. Wear the appropriate clothing when necessary; ideas on what to wear are shown below. In addition, if very noisy operations are being carried out, give serious consideration to wearing earplugs, to avoid damaging one's hearing. In the case of sensitive skin, use a suitable barrier cream that can prevent skin rashes or dermatitis caused by contact with fluxes and oils. All of this may sound rather formidable, but by and large it is only basic common sense. There is no need to go to excess in taking precautions, just ensure that sensible care is taken.

Tools and Machinery

All power tools and machines must be properly earthed, and where practical guards should be fitted. Often when machines are bought second-hand there are no guards, in which case it is advisable to organize some sort of shield. A sheet of perspex or similar material held to the machine with a couple of clips will at least make one aware of the danger. A guard on a machine frequently will serve the additional purpose of preventing swarf from flying all over the workshop, in particular when machining brass.

Most of the illustrations in this book will show operations that appear to be carried out on unguarded machinery. In fact, the guard will have been removed purely for the purpose of taking the photographs.

Leaving a chuck key like this is a source of real danger should the machine be started without its removal.

Above *A guard on a drilling machine, sufficient to prevent flying swarf from causing cuts. It should be emphasised that no guard is foolproof, and responsible behaviour is the best safety precaution of all.*

Above right *A guard such as this fitted over the chuck of a Cowell Lathe will not only help to prevent injury, but also prevents swarf from flying all over the place.*

Worn Tools Can be Dangerous

Avoid using files without handles or where the handles are split. Hammers are also a source of danger if the shafts are ill fitting or split or the head splayed out with wear.

However, there is nothing dangerous about old tools as long as they are well looked after and properly maintained. It pays to take good care of your tools.

CLOTHING

Boots and Shoes

In industry there are numerous regulations regarding the protective clothing that a worker should use. Some operations require the use of face masks, eye shields, special gloves, heavy boots and clothing that will offer protection from chemicals or heat. If metalworking is a hobby, nobody wants to spend half an hour putting on special clothing and then wandering around looking like an out of work spaceman. However, suitable precautions should be taken at the right time and the best place to start is at the bottom by using sensible footwear. Going into a metalworking environment wearing open-toed sandals or carpet slippers really is asking for trouble. Any heavy metal object that is dropped or falls off a bench appears to be programmed to find the nearest unprotected foot. Likewise, drop a pointed article and it will land point first; there may be a good scientific reason for this, but there surely cannot be one for the fact that it will invariably land on one's foot if only wearing carpet slippers. Wear good stout shoes or boots at all times.

Clothes

Overalls may be less important than good footwear; they are used mainly to prevent damage to normal clothing, and so must be a matter of individual preference.

Protection Against Heat

There are certain operations where it is wise to use some form of protective clothing, particularly if a lot of heat is to be used. Always remember that synthetic fibres are dangerous as they can, in extreme heat, melt and adhere to the skin.

Blacksmiths and workers in foundries and similar industries are banned from wearing shirts made of these materials, because of the danger involved. It could be worthwhile investing in a special apron if very hot work is undertaken. Do not in such circumstances try to work without any clothing as protection, as even being adjacent to very high temperatures can cause nasty burns.

Gloves

For some operations it is worthwhile protecting the hands by wearing gloves, as they offer protection from splinters and in some instances from heat. However, for practical reasons gloves cannot be worn at all times. A good stout and if possible heatproof pair should be available for use should they be required.

Eye Protection

For all machining operations safety spectacles or an eye shield be worn. Any type of machining can cause swarf to be thrown in the air, easily resulting in damage to the eyes. In particular, eye protection is absolutely essential when using a grinding machine of any sort.

For general work, safety spectacles such as these are ideal. They are fitted with clear lenses and small side flaps and are sufficient to prevent damage to the eyes during most normal workshop operations. It is possible to get prescription safety spectacles made if required.

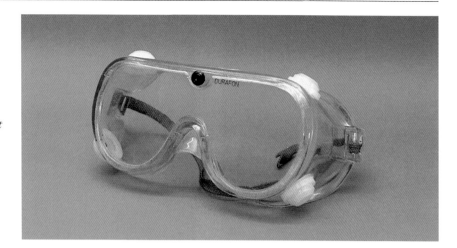

If a great deal of dust or shavings are anticipated it is best to wear a full eye mask such as this. It will also fit over spectacles if they are normally worn.

Face masks. The one on the right is successful against dust and fumes, providing the latter is not in heavy concentration. The one on the left has replaceable filters and is proof against all dust and fumes likely to be found in a home workshop.

Face Masks

For most work, a face mask will not be necessary, but sometimes cutting oils give off fumes that can cause an irritation to the throat, even if they might not actually be dangerous. Fluxes used for soldering also release irritating fumes and some silver solders release cadmium fumes that are really dangerous. In these circumstances, it is advisable to use a mask to cover the mouth and nose, although it only needs to be a comparatively simple one. Wearing an eye shield and face mask will invariably result in the eye shield steaming up and the operator not being in a position to see the work. Therefore instead of a shield use safety glasses. However, if a shield is essential because spectacles are worn, a mask that releases spent air through a filter at the front must be used. It is possible to get safety spectacles made that conform to the prescription of normal spectacles and these are far more convenient than trying to wear an eye shield in addition to normal glasses.

13

THE WORKSHOP PREMISES

The Garage

Probably the facility most frequently used as a workshop is the garage, and properly prepared it can be quite a good venue, especially if it is not to be shared with a car. However, most garages have a concrete floor and unlike houses are made from a single layer of material, most probably without a damp-proof membrane, which makes them very prone to condensation. If the car is also housed in the garage, then the problem is greatly exaggerated. Condensation of course invariably means that tools and machines will in no time be covered in rust, and so the first thing to consider is that if sharing with a car, some form of partition that will separate the workshop from the vehicle should if possible be erected. Ideally, this should be a substantial structure with some form of insulation – even 20mm or so of insulating material makes all the difference.

Insulation

The outer walls of a garage should be insulated by fitting battens and then nailing a suitable covering to them, putting insulating material between the covering and the walls. Polystyrene sheeting specially designed for this purpose is sold at builder's merchants and a minimum thickness of 20mm should be aimed for. This material has been fireproofed and is therefore safe to use. Be wary of economizing by using polystyrene from old packing cases and the like, as such materials may not have been suitably

---

Fitting Wall Cupboards

Because of the problem of holding objects securely to insulation board, some people like to use chipboard for cladding walls as it is strong enough to support smaller objects and shelves that are not going to be used for anything heavy. Even so, it is still advisable that shelves, cupboards and so on should be screwed right through into the wall.

---

treated. If in doubt, break a small piece off, take it outside and throw a lighted match on it – keep well clear, as the fumes are highly toxic. If it has been fireproofed the match will quickly go out, with the material showing only slight signs of charring; if not, it will quickly catch fire and release dense black smoke.

The roof should be dealt with in a similar manner to the walls, although generally there will be beams to which the cladding can be fitted. If the garage is made of brick or building blocks, the beams will be of wood and so fixing the cladding is simply a case of nailing it in position. Precast concrete garages as a rule have steel trusses instead of beams, which makes life a little more difficult as it will be necessary to make special brackets to support the material. Once again, insulation material such as polystyrene sheet or loft insulation material, which is sold in rolls, should be installed prior to fitting the cladding. It is also highly probable that it will be necessary to run electric cables through the roof space and these should be fitted before the cladding.

Cladding Materials

The purpose of the cladding material is both to insulate and to provide a nice finish, preferably one that can be painted. Insulation board is ideal, and is obtainable from builder's merchants. In particular, it is ideal for ceilings, but as it does not accept screws very successfully it will be necessary first of all to secure pieces of wood in the space above where the board will go so that the fittings can be attached to them. It follows that for retaining heat, insulation board is also the best material for the walls, but invariably shelves and cupboards will be required that need to be screwed to the wall. This requires careful planning as to where screws are to go, and once again it may be necessary to fit extra timbers that will take them.

At one time it was necessary to nail or screw cladding to battens, but it is now possible to get adhesives that are strong enough to do the job and these are worth considering. The only disadvantage in their use is that should it ever be necessary to remove the panelling, the task is almost impossible.

The Floor

The floor is a source of both damp and cold and it is advisable to cover a garage floor with a sheet of plastic to act as a damp-proof membrane, putting good quality flooring chipboard on top of that, which in turn can be either painted or tiled. A good alternative is to lay laminated flooring, used in conjunction with a special underlay that not only keeps out the damp but also provides some insulation from the cold. There is no reason why this type of underlay should not be used in conjunction with chipboard instead of a membrane, if the arrangement is found to be more suitable.

SECTIONAL BUILDINGS

Wooden Sheds

Another commonly used facility for a workshop is a wooden shed, more often than not purchased as a sectional building especially for the purpose. These make excellent workshops, but need to be insulated in the same way as a garage.

The wooden floor that is usually supplied with this type of building is also more often than not unsuitable for use where machinery is involved. Additional support should be fitted underneath in the form of joists and a layer of flooring quality chipboard put on top of the floor that is supplied. Between the floor and the chipboard put a layer of roofing felt, as generally speaking wooden sheds are not designed to keep out draughts and something is needed for warmth. A properly insulated shed makes a very warm and cosy workshop area and is well worth considering.

Precast Concrete Buildings

Garden buildings are also available that are made from precast concrete, and these are quite popular as workshops. One difficulty with a

---

Foundations

It is often the practice when a wooden shed is for garden use simply to lay paving stones or battens directly on the ground as a foundation. This will not be suitable for a building that is to house machinery; a proper foundation consisting of hardcore covered with a layer of concrete is necessary. The depth of the foundation will depend on local soil conditions and the area Building Inspector will be able to offer advice on the matter.

---

wooden building is the possibility of rot setting in after a number of years, which of course does not happen with concrete. However, these buildings are more prone to condensation than wood and must be treated in exactly the same manner as a garage as regards insulation.

A ROOM IN THE HOUSE

For pure comfort there is nothing as good as having a workshop installed in a room in the house. There is of course no need to worry about insulation, but even so it might be desirable to cover the walls with one of the modern plastic-coated hardboards for protection. All machines throw out quantities of oil and swarf that will quickly impregnate a plaster wall, and in the event of the owner wishing to sell the property it is impossible to paint or paper over these materials.

MAKE IT PORTABLE

Some people who are engaged in the lighter side of metalworking do not have a permanent space, but instead make up a portable unit that can be used on any table, or sometimes can be wheeled from place to place. A lathe, if one is needed, will be of the small table-top type and the vice generally one that clamps in position. The workshop, or perhaps we should call it a work table, is taken out as needed and put away out of sight when finished with. This idea is commonly used by people who for one reason or another have to live in small, confined quarters, and is also popular amongst disabled people who could not possibly make use of the facilities offered by a large workshop.

BASEMENTS

Many people living in older houses find the basement highly suitable as a place in which to work, although it can have a couple of disadvantages. Firstly, there is usually little, if any, natural light, and, secondly, it can be very difficult to get machinery down the stairs. That apart, a basement has the advantage of being very convenient, while at the same time not being in any way intrusive on the living quarters and yet with all the facilities of the house readily available.

LOFTS

Lofts provide similar facilities to basements, but it is even more difficult to get machinery into a loft. However, if one is doing light work, such as clock or jewellery making, it can be a useful area in which to work, but some insulation will be needed to prevent the space being too hot in summer and too cold in winter.

ELECTRICITY SUPPLIES

Whether or not someone chooses personally to fit the electricity supply to the workshop is down to individual experience in these matters. Many people setting up their own workshops will be well experienced in electrical installation and it would be wrong to suggest that they employ a contractor. However, it must be pointed out that machines consume a considerable amount of electrical current, and so if in any doubt, get a professional to do the job.

Single or Three Phase?

Some machines that are bought second-hand will be designed for three-phase supply at 415V, rather than the domestic supply. The local electricity company can install a three-phase supply to the home workshop if one wishes, although doing so is an expensive proposition. If it is to be a large workshop with a lot of heavy machinery, then possibly the three-phase supply is worth having, as the machines will start more readily and consume less current when running. However, with the type of machines sold specially with the small workshop in mind it is easier and more economical to use the ordinary single-phase supply. But there is always the situation where one wishes to purchase a single machine fitted with a three-phase motor and it is not economical to have a suitable electrical supply installed. In such cases, special adaptors known as Rotary Phase Converters usually work out considerably cheaper than installing a three-phase supply, although they can have limitations on the amount of current that can be drawn from them. Nevertheless, they are worth investigating. The alternative is to change the motor for a single-phase type.

Fuses

A consumer unit, more commonly known as a fuse box, should definitely be fitted in all workshops, as switching on and off electrical motors that power machines creates a short but very heavy surge of current. This surge could not only cause domestic fuses to blow, but if the household wiring is in any way faulty a fire could result. The workshop supply should be taken from the household supply to a consumer unit, using a cable rated at 30 amps as used for electric cookers. The unit in the workshop should be of the type that trips, rather than one where fuse wire disintegrates if the current consumed is too heavy. From the unit at least two supplies will be needed, a higher rated one that will go to sockets into which machinery will be plugged, and a lower rated one for lighting; the latter need only be 5 amps, but the power should be rated at 16 amps. Both circuits should be in the form of a ring, which means that they return to the consumer unit after having passed to all the outlets.

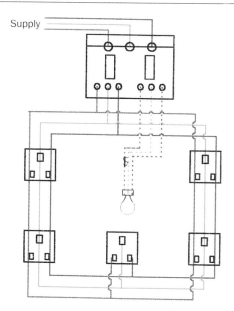

Supply

Suggested ring circuit for a small workshop.
Lighting circuit wiring is shown as dotted lines.

The layout of a ring circuit.

Electrical Supplies Outside

In many cases, installing electricity will mean taking it outside the environment of the house and running a cable into the garden. All such cables should be kept as short as possible. The cable used for outside supplies should always be of the armoured type or carried inside a metal conduit; if it is being run underground it must be at a depth of at least 46cm (18in), and in a trench that is lined with gravel that will allow drainage. It is actually preferable to line the trench with tiles or some form of ducting, so that the cable is not lying in the earth. There is no objection to an armoured cable running along a brick or stone wall, but it should be supported at intervals of no more than 200mm (8in) by suitable clamps. Under no circumstances should a cable be run along a wooden fence.

Overhead Cables

Sometimes it will be necessary to take the cable overhead. It is difficult to generalize on exactly how this should be done as every situation differs, but it is essential that the cable be firmly fitted to the wall of the house from whence it

comes, using insulated clamps held with at least four screws. The distance of travel overhead should be kept to a minimum and the support post at the far end should be of metal, cemented into the ground. Wooden posts rot and it is not always possible to tell that this has happened, so it is very dangerous to use wood in case at some time in the future the post might collapse, bringing with it a live electrical cable. It goes without saying that the height of the cable must be sufficient to allow someone to carry a tall object, such as a ladder, underneath without fouling. A general guide would be about 3m (10ft).

LIGHTING

Thought should be given to the layout of the workshop and as much use as possible made of daylight. It is possibly better to have a bench near the window rather than the lathe or milling machine, but it is really a matter of personal choice. Good lighting is essential for good workmanship and as well as adequate overhead lighting, all machines and the bench should have some form of individual lighting.

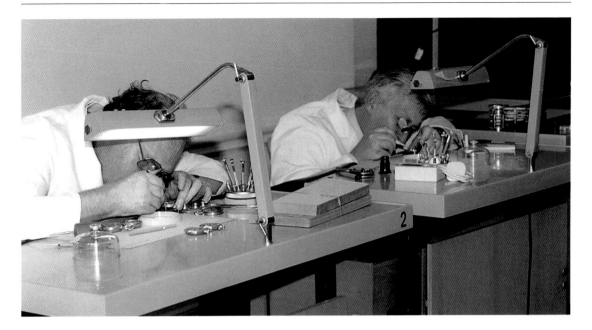

The best for this purpose is the low-voltage halogen individual lamp, as this directs a good bright light to the exact area where it is wanted, while being small enough not to be intrusive. Like most things, the form of overhead lighting employed is a matter of individual

Above *A scene in the watchmaking workshop of the British Horological Society, showing how the use of good quality lighting assists the workmen.*

choice. Some people prefer the ordinary tungsten type, but most appear to prefer fluorescent lighting, in which case the best type of tube to use is the one called daylight, rather than that referred to as white.

HEATING

The type of heating must be carefully chosen, as anything that carries a direct gas flame will cause condensation and in no time at all create havoc by the amount of rust it will leave on tools and machines. Unless a radiator from the domestic central heating is installed in the workshop, we are more or less therefore confined to some form of electric heating, or a coal-fired stove. There are numerous types of electric devices available, from radiators to fan heaters, all of which seem to work quite well, and we should not forget the night-storage

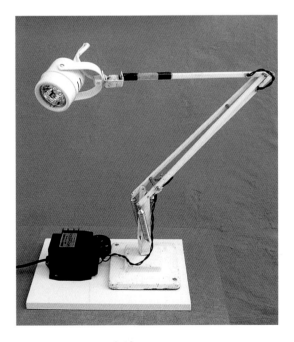

Left *A low-voltage halogen bench-standing lamp, which is ideal for localized lighting.*

18

heater that uses cheap electricity with which to maintain heat in the workshop throughout the day. The small, enclosed coal stove has now largely gone out of fashion, and yet it has the advantage that it radiates a good amount of heat, some of which is retained after the fire has gone out, thereby avoiding rapid cooling and the main cause of condensation. It is also possible to use such a stove for heat treatment of metals, thus killing two birds with one stone.

EQUIPMENT

The Bench

Unless you happen to be one of those people who has to make use of portable equipment, the first requisite of a workshop is a good strong bench. Although it is nice to have a very large one, in some ways this can be self-defeating, as any flat surface inevitably becomes a repository for bits and pieces and leads to clutter. A good maximum size to aim for is about 600mm (2ft) in depth, with a length of about twice that size. However, in most cases circumstances will dictate the size, as the bench will be built to fit the space available. The height of the bench is extremely important, and over the years it has become generally acknowledged that the ideal height is one that, when standing, the elbow will be level with the top of the vice.

Bench Tops

It matters little whether the frame is made of wood or metal as long as the bench is sturdy; to add support it should if possible be bolted to the wall of the workshop. The top too needs to be substantial, and obtaining wood of a suitable quality and thickness is not easy these days, particularly as ideally hardwood should be used. A compromise is therefore necessary, and there are several ways of doing this. Well-seasoned planks can be laid side by side and the top covered with either chipboard or hardboard that is subsequently well varnished in order to prevent the soaking in of any liquid that might be spilled on it. Alternatively, several layers of outdoor quality plywood can be glued together to make a single board that needs to be about 40mm (1.5in) thick; again the top and edges must be well sealed and varnished to prevent dampness from penetrating. Thick block board was once a firm favourite for making bench tops and is still a good choice, but hardwood strips must be used to cover the edges if it is used.

The Bench Vice

Most tools that will be required for various operations will be dealt with in the chapters devoted to those particular aspects of things, a few however must be regarded as general all purpose items and one of these is the vice. The

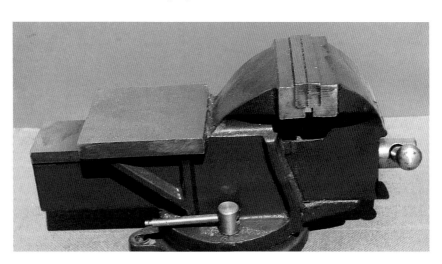

A bench vice with built-in anvil.

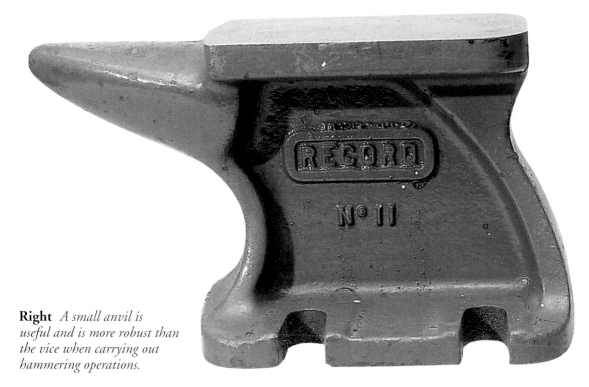

Right *A small anvil is useful and is more robust than the vice when carrying out hammering operations.*

Below *A swivelling engineering vice.*

engineering vice differs from the one used by a woodworker, where the vice is fitted to the side of the bench. An engineers' vice is bolted to the top and bolted should be the optimum word as it is never a good idea to fit it with wood screws. Hacksawing and filing, not to mention operations such as bending and riveting put a tremendous strain on it and in no time at all wood screws will work loose.

Selecting the Size
The size of vice chosen will depend to some extent on the work to be done, but it is advisable always to get one as large as possible. If heavy iron work is to be the order of the day a vice with jaws at least 100mm (4in) in width will be needed. For more general work 75mm (3in) will suffice, although 100mm will do no harm. If light work only is being under taken then nothing with jaws of a greater width than 50mm (2in) will be required. It must always be borne in mind that a vice is not indestructible and as all, except the most expensive, are made from cast iron, it is only too easy to break them by misuse. In general therefore, any hammering should be carried out at the top of the jaws where there is most metal and should be kept as light as possible. If there is to be any heavy hammering, a small anvil should be kept for the purpose. It is possible to buy one that will stand on a bench, although if room is not a problem there is nothing better than a full-sized floor-standing anvil for this sort of work. If the vice must be used to hold work for hammering, this must never take place on the movable section that protrudes, as this is the weakest point. A vice can be obtained that has a flat plate cast into its construction, which protects that weak point and is designed to take a limited amount of hammering. As such, this makes a good compromise between the anvil and vice.

Some vices have quick-release mechanisms, whereby pulling a lever releases the nut on the lead screw and takes the pressure from the work. These are mainly designed for use in places where time is important and there is no great advantage in having one in a home

workshop. It is also possible to obtain a vice on a swivel base that allows it to be turned, thereby sometimes making a more convenient angle at which to work. These can be very useful, although there is a very slight loss of rigidity with this type of vice.

Soft Jaws
The jaws on the majority of vices are deliberately made as hard as possible to allow them to grip the work, but this also has the effect of badly marking and possibly even damaging it. Special protecting devices that slip over the jaws can be bought, or alternatively pieces of zinc may be hammered over to do the same job. Another alternative is to use short pieces of aluminium angle. If a lot of work is to be done where there is concern that the metal should not be marked, it is quite easy to remove the hard jaws, which are held in

An aluminium angle used to protect work from damage by vice jaws.

Plain mild steel jaws used to replace the normal hardened ones in order to protect the work.

place by two countersunk screws, and replace them with plain mild steel blocks. In some cases, these are better than the usual type of removable soft jaw, particularly if there is precision filing to be carried out, as they are held securely in place. The removable type can lift as they close, making it difficult to see the position of the marks that are used as a guide to cutting and filing.

Machine Vices

A different type of vice is used for operations involving drilling and milling; it has a flat base and lugs that enable it to be bolted to the milling or drilling table. This type of vice is available in a variety of sizes and qualities and generally speaking the cheaper ones of a very basic construction should be confined to holding work for drilling only.

A typical machine vice used for drilling and milling operations. This example is home-made and is an interesting project to make.

STORAGE

Everyone will have their own storage problems to deal with, and no two people will find the same solution. It is essential that tools and materials are kept in places where it is convenient to get at them, and to a large extent this will depend on how the workshop is built and equipped, but some general suggestions can be made.

Storing Metal Sections

The storage of strip metal of any profile can be difficult, particularly as over a period of years one tends to collect large quantities of the stuff, all in varying lengths. Standing it on end in a corner is all right when there is not a lot of it, but once the quantity increases it becomes something of a nightmare searching through the pile to find the piece required. One answer is to use lengths of ordinary guttering bolted to the wall and to lay the metal in those in some sort of order. Another useful alternative is to use drainpiping. The latter can be either stood on end or laid on a substantial shelf on the wall, where it will be found that the lengths of piping nestle into each other, making a compact storage system. For short lengths of metal stored in piping, make up wooden plugs to fit the ends so that the metal does not fall out when the piping is picked up.

Sheet metal will generally need to be stored

A storage shelf fitted over a lathe headstock. It is a great space-saving idea and contains all the tools likely to be needed for that machine.

in a vertical position and should be kept at as near to 90 degrees as possible in order to prevent warping. It can be held against a wall or the side of a bench by fitting two small hooks and running plastic-covered curtain-hanging wire between them. Small pieces of sheet metal should be laid flat on a shelf.

The space under the bench can be used for storage purposes, and even if the workshop is large enough for this not to be a necessity it is still worthwhile making storage facilities for certain frequently needed items. Most of the tools required in metalworking are quite small, and so if possible use small drawers or cupboards with shelves – if they can be purpose-made for the tools they will hold, so much the better. Even when things are kept on shelves or in a cupboard under the bench it is better to make suitable boxes to house them, rather than have them just pushed in anywhere.

Because of the weight they are likely to carry, cupboards must be either floor-standing or firmly fixed, preferably with brackets or a wooden batten underneath in addition to any other means of securing them. Thought should be given to the position of any partitions in order that they can be used to their maximum capacity. Shelving likewise needs to be firmly fixed, and a good idea is to drill holes to accept certain tools, so that the shelf does dual duty as a rack as well as a shelf. This particularly applies to shelves that might be fitted near machinery and therefore used to store tooling with Morse

Tapers, and so on. A chuck, for example, stored by a Morse Taper pushed through a hole in a shelf, will take up far less space than if it is laid on the shelf.

Screwdrivers can be held to a flat surface by pushing them into spring clips and it is a good idea to use the inside of cupboard doors for this purpose, thus using space that would otherwise be wasted. Hacksaws and other types of saws can also be stored on the inside of cupboard doors on hooks. If possible, taps and dies should not be kept in boxes and allowed to rub together, as in no time at all the cutting edge will become blunted. Proper trays should be made for them, or alternatively they can be kept in wooden blocks with holes drilled in them. If for some reason it is essential to store them in boxes, wrap the threads in insulating tape to prevent them from being damaged.

Angled Shelves

When shelves are fitted in the normal way in the immediate vicinity of machinery such as lathes, it is a good idea to set them at an angle of about 20 degrees, otherwise in no time at all they will become heavily laden with swarf. Tools can be retained on them either by pushing them into holes as outlined in the section on storing metal, or by making suitable brackets with which to hold them.

An angled shelf, designed with the intention that swarf would fall off it, also stops unwanted items being left on it.

Right *The inside of cupboard door used for storage of screwdrivers and similar tools.*

Below *A narrow tool cupboard, used mainly for housing hacksaws. Wooden templates have been made that make it easier to replace tools and ensure that only those intended to be stored are there.*

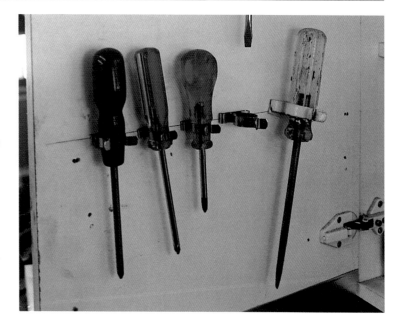

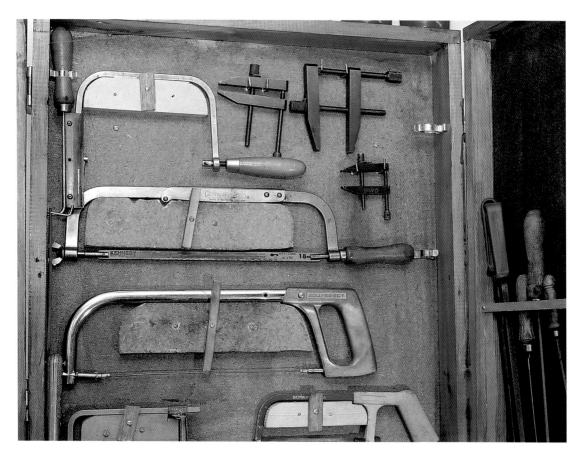

Small tools kept together in simple hardwood blocks with holes drilled in them.

Tool Boxes

It is tempting to buy or make a nice big toolbox in which to keep small tools, but this is not always such a good idea. Invariably as the tool collection grows, the toolbox becomes very heavy and difficult to move about. Although it might be possible to find a corner in which to keep the toolbox, so that it is out of the way, it will still be necessary to open it in order to get the tools out and extra space has to be found in which the lid can be swung open. Frequently there are trays that have to be taken out in order to get at certain tools that are in the bottom of the box; the result is a clutter all over the floor and not only does the workshop become a mess but an unnecessary hazard has been created. Toolboxes therefore are best kept fairly small and used only as means of transporting tools, or for storing items that will only be used on very rare occasions.

KEEP THE WORKSHOP CLEAN AND TIDY

In theory at least, at the end of a working session all tools should be put away and any swarf, dust and so on cleaned up. Machines should be wiped down and unpainted surfaces given a light coating of oil to prevent rust forming. However, despite the obvious benefits of such a routine, if followed to the letter there would be no time to do any work! It may be found best to set oneself certain priorities, starting by making sure that small items, such as drills, taps, dies and reamers, are put in their proper places. These things easily get mislaid or covered with odds and ends as well as swarf,

---

A Tidy Bench

A big aid to keeping a bench tidy is to make sure that when tools are laid on it they are all facing the same way, although not necessarily at 90 degrees to the edge. If they are just put down anyhow, the bench soon becomes a mass of jumble and this is when small items become hard to find.

A useful storage system for small items can be made from old 35mm film containers set into a wooden frame like this.

soon becoming almost impossible to find. It is also a good idea to make it a priority to clear away swarf and apply a little oil to surfaces, particularly if the workshop is not used on a regular basis. Otherwise, have regular clearing up sessions so that it is possible not only to keep the workshop tidy, but also to keep track of where everything is.

Keep a Log

Workshops tend to expand, or at least the tools and equipment do. In general, metalworking tools do not wear out and if taken care of will last for many years, so as new things are bought, made or perhaps received as presents, the amount of equipment increases and it becomes harder to recall where everything is kept. There is nothing more frustrating than deciding to have a working session, only to spend most of the time available looking for that little thingamabob that was put carefully away a couple of months earlier, but exactly where just cannot be recalled. One way to prevent this is to keep a notebook with a record of where everything is stored and if the storage place changes to make sure that the entry in the notebook is also changed. Another option is to make a card index that is screwed to the wall. It should carry two columns of cards, one showing the item, the other where it is stored. All cards are removable and if the storage place of an item is changed a replacement card is inserted.

2 Working Materials

METALS

It is considered normal that a carpenter or cabinetmaker should have knowledge of the properties of the wood to be used for a particular task; indeed, without that knowledge the end result could be a disaster. He wants to know how hard the wood is, how straight the grain is and its properties when sawn, planed and chiselled. Unfortunately many who take up metalworking have no similar knowledge of the metal they propose to use, and yet similar factors apply. Metal has a grain and hardness, as well as machining and finishing properties, about which we should know something, while not expecting to be a metallurgist. All metals used nowadays are alloys containing small percentages of other metals, which results in a wide range of materials, suitable for every purpose. In general, we will be looking for the metal that can be adapted for use in as many circumstances as possible. Most, if not all, readers will know the difference between steel, aluminium and brass, but there are many variations of each of these, each designed for a specific purpose. Unless engaged in specific work, requiring a certain standard, it is usually a case of using whatever grade is best suited to one's needs, rather trying to obtain a special formula.

Properties of Metals					
Metal	Uses	Heat Treatment	Availability	Machining	Comments
Cast iron	Bearings Castings	None.	As cast or in rough bars	Easy but with hard skin. Definitely not to be lubricated.	Creates dust when worked. Accepts paint.
Mild steel	General fabrications	Some types can be case hardened. Can be soft soldered, brazed and welded.	All shapes and many sizes. Obtainable as bright or black.	Varies with quality, needs supply of cutting oil. Can be bent and sheet can be folded.	Useful for many purposes. Swarf varies from continuous spirals to chips. Accepts paint well.

Metal	Uses	Heat Treatment	Availability	Machining	Comments
Properties of Metals *continued*					
Carbon steel	Shafts, valves, etc. Higher carbon types useful for tools	Most types can be hardened and tempered. All can be brazed and welded.	Bar, round and flat stock. Stocked only by specialist tool suppliers.	Generally quite hard, needs good supply of lubricant. Carbide-tipped tools recommended.	Swarf usually short. Will accept paint.
Copper	Ornamental work and pressure vessels	Can be annealed but soon work-hardens. Takes soft and hard solder particularly well.	Sheet, bar and tube.	Difficult. Hardens as operations are carried out. Lubrication with white spirit can help. Do not use cutting oils. Can be bent and rolled.	Swarf is hard with very sharp edges. Does not accept paint very well.
Brass	Ornamental work. Bearings, general construction	Can be annealed, but care needed to avoid distortion. Takes soft and hard solders very well.	Sheet and rods, all forms of bars as well as tubes.	Very easy, needs no lubrication. Some forms can be bent and rolled.	Swarf discharged as fine spray that flies everywhere. Needs special primers for successful painting. Cheaper forms not suitable for use where contact with hot water required.
Bronze	Mainly bearings	Does not easily anneal and some types work-harden. Most forms can be soft or hard soldered.	Generally as rods or bars of various shapes. Can be obtained as oil-impregnated bearings.	Varies considerably with type of bronze. Some easy machining types are available. Lubrication with white spirit, not cutting oils.	Considerable variation in swarf discharge because there are so many types of bronze. Needs special primer for painting.

continued overleaf

		Properties of Metals *continued*			
Metal	Uses	Heat Treatment	Availability	Machining	Comments
Gunmetal	Bearings and castings	Cannot be hardened or annealed. Can be soft and hard soldered.	Usually only in cast form.	Very easy, but sometimes can be quite sticky. No lubrication required.	Short lengths of swarf. Needs special primer for painting.
Nickel silver	General fabrication	Can be annealed, work-hardens. Accepts soft and hard solders.	Sheet and small section bars and rods.	Very easy, no lubrication required.	Swarf in short lengths. Accepts paint easily and well.
Aluminium and alloys bases thereon	Castings and general fabrication	Work-hardens. Difficult to anneal. Can be soldered by using special techniques.	Sheet, rods and bars as well as extrusions.	Easy, but metal builds up on tool, making constant attention to clear cutting edge necessary. Lubrication with white spirit.	Swarf varies according to type of alloy, can be sharp and in long lengths. Needs special primer for painting.

CAST IRON

The most basic of all the ferrous metals is iron, which we will usually come into contact with in the form of castings that have been specially cast to the basic shape that we want. If a particular shape is not needed it is possible to buy iron in bar form, which has been cast but by a different method. Bars of iron usually have a smoother surface than cast components, which have generally been cast in sand moulds, with the result that some of the sand adheres to the surface, creating a very hard outer shell that does not generally exist on bar stock. The machining properties of a bar of iron are also frequently superior to that of a casting, which can suffer from two defects. The first is blowholes, of varying sizes, which are caused by the metal not flowing smoothly through the mould and leaving holes. The second problem can be that of chilled sections, which are created when the casting is tipped on to a cold concrete floor before it has cooled sufficiently in the mould. It is virtually impossible to machine through these hard spots, and the only cure is to heat the casting to red hot and keep it at that temperature for a very long time, before allowing it to cool slowly. For blowholes there is no real cure; the hole is there and that is that. If it is not in a vital position, such as the bore of a cylinder, it may be possible to fill the hole with a proprietary filler, such as an epoxy resin, mixed with plenty of cast-iron dust. If so, it will be barely visible, although it will not have any great wearing properties. Suppliers and founders recognize these problems and are invariably willing to replace castings with either of these faults. Unfortunately, blowholes seem to be able to keep themselves hidden until the work is nearly complete and then show up, meaning that all the work has to be done again.

Cast iron is magnetic, has good wearing properties when used for bearing surfaces, and accepts paint well. It is a surprisingly soft

A founder preparing to cast a specific iron component in a sand mould. The sand is first sifted to ensure that it will flow nicely around the pattern.

material once the outer skin has been penetrated and will harden during machining, particularly if a coolant is used, and so should always be machined dry. It is also inclined to twist and warp after machining. This occurs because the outer shell contains the stresses inside and as soon as it is removed, even partially, the inner stresses take hold. One way to avoid the problem is to leave any cast iron in a place where it is exposed to the weather, so that it goes rusty, which has the effect of relieving the stress and it will no longer distort.

31

The sand is rammed down as hard as possible, the pattern is removed and the molten metal poured in.

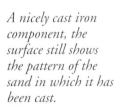

A nicely cast iron component, the surface still shows the pattern of the sand in which it has been cast.

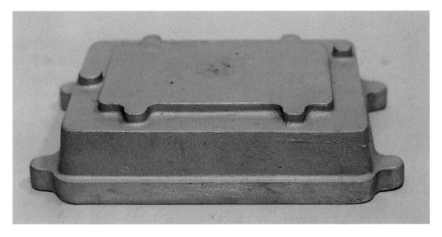

STEEL

Mild Steels

All modern metals, including steel, are alloys and all steel contains a certain amount of carbon. Generally steel used in the home workshop can be divided into four sections: bright mild, black mild, high-carbon and stainless. There are further subdivisions, particularly for high-carbon and bright mild steels. If the percentage of carbon is less than 0.25, it is generally designated as mild steel. As far as bright mild and black mild steels are concerned the names basically sum things up – when purchased one is bright and shiny, the other is a dull black colour. Mild steels are available in bar or sheet form and bar stock is available as round, hexagonal, rectangular and square as well as angles, tubes and other shapes, in a very wide variety of both metric and imperial sizes. High-carbon steel is generally only available in bar or flat section. Mild steel is not suitable for heat treatment, such as hardening and tempering, but can be case-hardened and special grades are obtainable that are specially designed for the purpose.

The photograph shows left: bright mild steel; middle: high-carbon steel; right: black mild steel.

Black Mild Steel

In general, compared to bright material black mild steel tends to be a little more stable and less inclined to distort after machining. It is also easier for marking out, as a scriber point will go through the black surface, leaving a nice bright line. The main objection to its use is the difficulty in getting a shiny finish, as a lot of work is involved in cleaning off the hard black surface. Nor does the process by which it is made leave sharp corners on rectangular section in the same way that the process used to make bright mild steel does. Black mild takes paint well, is a good material to work with and is used extensively in cases where one would many years ago have used wrought iron. It is very suitable for artistic work, particularly as it is easy to weld and braze.

Bright Mild Steel

Bright mild is generally more popular black mild, particularly for machining, as it is easy to obtain a nice finish. It is available in a whole range of specifications that generally relate to its ease of working; if possible, check what the specification is before purchasing, to ensure that it will be suitable. For example, free-machining steel will contain a small quantity of lead that is added during manufacture to help the free-machining process; it also has the advantage of increasing the life of machine tools, as well as allowing work to be completed more quickly. However, it does not have the same tensile strength as a harder grade and is less suitable for a component that will be subject to wear. While the inclusion of lead does make bright mild steels easy to machine and polish, they are almost impossible to braze or silver solder and cannot be case-hardened.

Case-Hardening Steel

While many types of mild steel can be case-hardened, a process that involves impregnating the outer skin with carbon, there are a number of types of steel that are specially manu-factured to aid the process. Case-hardening steels are bright and are generally not easily distinguishable from free-cutting steel (they have a slightly duller finish, but this is hardly noticeable). Because of this, any case-hardening quality steel that is obtained should either be clearly marked as such, or kept separate from other bright mild, in order not to select the wrong material for a job. The case-hardening quality steels are generally slightly more difficult to work with, as they are harder than other forms of mild steel. However, that extra little bit of hardness makes them suitable in many instances where free-cutting steel would be considered too soft and black undesirable on account of its colour. Should there be the need to obtain a larger piece than is normally sold at tool suppliers, it is best to pay a visit to a local scrapyard and obtain an old half shaft that can be machined to size.

High-Carbon Steel

In general, a percentage of 0.3 carbon will make the metal tough and ensure that it can easily be case-hardened, but it will not be suitable for normal hardening methods to be used. A percentage of 0.5 or higher is required to make the metal suitable for this type of hardening, and it is then used for making tools as well as work that will be put under a great deal of stress. Because of its ability to withstand stresses, high-carbon steel is extensively used in the motorcar industry for making crankshafts, half shafts, and valves. As far as the home metalworker is concerned, he or she will usually only need to use this sort of metal when making tools, and fortunately it can be obtained in small sections for this purpose. Special grades can be obtained by ordering them from a major stockist, although it is most unlikely that there will ever be a need to do this. High-carbon steel is also available in wire form for making springs. It is sometimes sold already hardened and tempered, and is also sold in its annealed form.

Special Tool Steels

Frequently, steel will be needed especially to make tools, perhaps a punch or a turning tool,

even possibly a tap or die for a special thread. High-carbon steels manufactured for this purpose can be bought as silver steel or ground flat stock, otherwise called gauge plate. Of the two, silver steel has the lower percentage of carbon and is only sold as round bar, while gauge plate is available as round bar or rectangular section. Both can be obtained in a variety of sizes and both have a ground finish that means they are very accurately sized and can also be used with confidence for measuring purposes. These two products are well proven and have been used by engineers for many years with success. At the same time, because they are sold in their annealed state, they are easy to use and can be machined or filed prior to hardening and tempering.

Special Quality Steels

High-speed steel is used by manufacturers of small tools, such as drills, taps, milling cutters and so on, for which it is specially designed. It is available as plain square or round section of various sizes in short lengths, intended for use as turning tools. When purchased, it has already gone through a special hardening and tempering process that gives it extra strength. It also gives it greater resistance to heat than ordinary high-carbon steel that has been hardened and tempered in the normal fashion. Because it arrives in the hardened state it cannot be machined or filed and tools made from it have to be ground to shape. As most small tools are made of it, a good source of short pieces is the remains of broken taps and milling cutters, the shanks of which can be ground and put into holders to make very acceptable turning tools. For even greater strength and durability high-speed steel is sometimes alloyed with other materials such as cobalt, vanadium and tungsten.

Stainless Steel

We are all familiar with stainless steel as it is used nowadays for a whole variety of domestic purposes. It is steel to which a number of elements, including chromium, have been added and it finds its uses in the home workshop where resistance to corrosion is important. Not all stainless steels are truly resistant to rust and a general rule is that the tougher the material is to work with, the more corrosion-resistant it will be. The anti-corrosion properties depend on the percentages of the materials used to make the steel. It is possible to get a rough idea of the resistance qualities of the steel by testing it with a magnet – the less a magnet attracts it, the less it is likely to rust. It cannot be hardened and tempered and is of no use for making tools, but it is tougher than mild steel and because of this tools used to work on it are subject to rapid wear. It is very difficult material to hard solder or weld, and for the latter the welding process is carried out through a film of inert gas.

NON-FERROUS METALS

Copper
Distinguishable by its reddish colour, copper is in particular used by model engineers for boiler-making, as it conducts heat rapidly and does not rust. Copper is also very good for ornamental work and is generally easy to cut,

drill and form into shapes, although it work-hardens very quickly. It is available as sheet, as well as square and round bar and tube. Rivets made from copper are very popular, both for their ability to form shape easily and their attractive appearance; it is a particularly easy material to soft or hard solder and although it tends to harden quickly it is very easy to anneal.

Bronze
A mixture of copper and tin produces the alloy known as bronze and because the composition of the alloy varies so does the colour. This can sometimes make it difficult to identify, as some bronzes appear very similar to brass. Generally, it is used for bearing surfaces and other situations where a tough material that is non-rusting is needed. It is available in round, square and hexagonal bar form. Machining qualities depend on the specification of the metal; some free-machining types are available, while other forms can be very difficult to work with, as they are extremely hard. With the addition of a very small percentage of zinc, bronze becomes gunmetal and is used to make

Copper is available as sheet bar or tube and is distinguishable by its rich red colour.

Brass is available in a whole variety of shapes and is yellow in colour, shades may vary according to the specification of the material.

castings. In this form it is softer than most ordinary bronzes and is easy to machine, although some types tend to be rather sticky. Sometimes aluminium is added to bronze in order to obtain better resistance to corrosion. This type of material is often used where there is likely to be contact with seawater, such as drilling platforms. It is also useful for bearings, but unlike the more usual forms of bronze cannot be hard or soft soldered. Some, but by no means all, of the bronzes designed to machine easily contain lead, and while their machining properties are superb and they will accept soft solder very well, the high temperatures involved in hard soldering cause the lead to leach out and prevent the formation of a joint.

Brass

An alloy of copper and zinc, brass has a wide variety of uses. It is easily distinguishable by its yellow colour and is available as sheet, all forms of bar, angles, round and square tubing and other shapes. It is generally very easy to work with, although it will work-harden. Some sheet brasses have a high percentage of zinc that makes them very easy to bend. These are of a light, almost silvery colour, and are not generally suitable for work involving machining. They also have a much lower melting point than the harder forms, and so this form of brass is frequently used to make domestic fittings such as hinges and door furniture. The addition of even more zinc results in a metal known as 60/40 Brass or Muntz Metal, which has a very low melting point indeed and is useful for filling tubing in order to prevent it kinking when bending, where more than a single bend in a short section is required. It can also be used for making simple castings, the low melting point enabling it to be poured into moulds made from silicone. Apart from these two examples, brass is an excellent material for hard or soft soldering. It can also be used for casting and is particularly useful where fine detail is needed, as it is very suitable for the process known as lost-wax casting.

Readers interested in clock-making should note that a special brass known as engraving brass is advisable as it has better wearing properties. Because zinc leaches out after a period of time, it is wise to avoid trying to use old brass fittings from scrapyards. One reason they may have been discarded is because they have become porous, and while initially the brass will appear to be in good condition it will rapidly deteriorate into a powder.

Gilding Metal

Gilding metal is a form of brass, although just a touch darker in colour. It is a particularly ductile metal that is used extensively for beaten metalwork. It can be formed into complex shapes, and any blemishes made in the process are easily removed. It is very easy to cut, does not work-harden and will accept hard and soft solder very well. Gilding metal is only available in sheet form.

Nickel Silver

A member of the family of brasses, this metal is a pleasant silvery colour and is a firm favourite with makers of artistic artefacts. Unlike gilding metal, it does not take kindly to forming by hammering, although it does bend easily. It is supplied in sheet or rod form, and in spite of the fact that it is easily bent is quite hard. It solders particularly well, with little oxidization, and accepts paint without the need for a special etching primer. For these reasons it is also a particular favourite of model-makers.

Aluminium

Aluminium is familiar to us all as the material from which both domestic saucepans and aeroplanes are made, but of course they are not actually made from anything like the same material. The name is commonly used for any of the numerous alloys based on aluminium, all of which have vastly differing properties. Overall, aluminium alloys are prized for both their lightness and non-rusting properties. They are ideal for jobs where excessive weight could be a problem. The alloys vary between being very soft and very hard, and some of those known under the name duralumin have great strength. Although aluminium can be annealed, it will harden again if left at room temperature for a week or so. Most of the alloys machine well, but have a tendency to build up deposits on tools. This is because of their low melting point, which results in minute particles of melted metal joining together and forming a solid piece, in turn welding itself to the cutting tool. Fabrications are usually joined by riveting or bolting parts together. Aluminium is available as sheet, bar or angle, or as castings, and is used for making specially shaped extrusions for shop fitting and domestic purposes, which can sometimes find a use in the workshop.

Aluminium is of a white to silver appearance and can be obtained as sheet, bar or extrusions. It is also frequently used for casting components such as this crank case for an engine.

PLASTICS

The modern engineer and therefore the metalworker will invariably find the need to use plastics of one sort or another, and there is now such a wide range available that the subject is a science of its own. Most of the material will not be of a great deal of use in the small workshop, but mention should be made of the few that are. Nylon is ideal for bearings where there is no excessive heat, as it is free running and requires no lubrication. Teflon will serve a similar purpose, and as well as being available in solid form can be obtained as a spray, which is very useful for lubrication. PTFE is particularly useful for making watertight seals and is no doubt familiar in tape form as used by plumbers. It is also available as rod and can be made into washers that provide an excellent water or steam seal. It can also be used to make piston rings, although allowance must be made for the fact it expands when heated. **Particular care must be taken when machining plastics, as the fumes can be highly toxic, especially if they are overheated.**

HEAT TREATMENT

Mention has already been made a number of times of the need to soften or harden metals; this means changing the molecular structure and involves the application of heat. Temperatures required will in some cases be nearing 1,000°C, although fortunately in general only a small amount of heat will be needed. To explain heat quantity, compare the heat of a bonfire made of wood and a lighted match. Both will reach similar temperatures, but the bonfire will have a far greater volume of heat than the match. In industry nowadays, metal is heated to the necessary temperature in an electric oven, which is very well insulated and capable of easily reaching these high temperatures. However, although it is not too difficult to construct such an oven for oneself, only those with a good working knowledge of electrical equipment should attempt to do so.

A blowlamp that is fitted directly to a gas canister. This size is sufficient to harden and temper small tools, but for large areas of metal a much larger lamp would be required.

Most people are content to use a blowlamp for hardening and tempering metal, and provided care is taken this is a very successful method.

Blowlamps

The first essential is a good blowlamp, the size of which will depend on the work that is to be carried out, as heating metal to high temperatures not only requires a blowlamp capable of reaching a high temperature, but it must also supply a sufficient quantity of heat at that temperature.

Dissipation of Heat

We see many small blowlamps advertised as having the ability to deliver a heat of nearly 2,000°C, and indeed they will do so, but the quantity of heat is so minute that as soon as it strikes the metal it is conducted away and so the metal will never reach the required temperature.

A hot bench being used to anneal a sheet of copper. The metal has been packed well round with reflective firebrick, which is being heated with a large gas torch, fuelled from a separate propane cylinder.

If only small work such as making jewellery is undertaken, these tiny lamps will be adequate, as there will not be sufficient metal to conduct the heat away, and to use anything larger would be fraught with danger. Larger work will need a correspondingly larger source of heat, and sometimes there may be a need to include a flow of oxygen to the flame in order to get the quantity of heat at the required temperature. Some blowlamps are available that are self-contained with a gas canister and these are fine for making small tools and so on, but if large areas of metal are to be heated a lamp that connects to a separate gas cylinder via a flexible pipe is desirable. The dispersal of heat through conductivity must always be taken into account and this will be greater with copper alloys than it is with steel, meaning that a larger heat source will be needed.

A Hot Bench

It is obvious that if a large amount of heat is to be used and the work is lying on a wooden bench, in no time at all there will be no workshop left and the fire brigade will be in attendance. A special hot bench is therefore a necessity. Although called a hot bench, in fact it needs to be only a small area just a little larger than the size of the work to be heated and should consist of some form of metal tray or dish filled with a heat-reflective material. Special bricks can be obtained that can be used for the purpose. Alternatively, use a deep layer of ceramic material, such as broken gas fire elements. If using bricks, make sure that they are of the reflective type – the ones sold for lining ordinary household fireplaces absorb rather than reflect heat, and this means that considerably more heat must be applied. Special silicone bricks are available, but may be difficult to find. A good compromise if nothing else is available is a thermolite block, which can be bought at any builder's merchant.

Any sort of steel tray can be used as a container. Old baking trays work quite well, or alternatively a special one can be folded from sheet metal, in which case the back can be raised up and lined, giving the advantage that the heat will be reflected back on the work. The tray must be on some form of legs or blocks to keep it clear of the bench, otherwise the heat generated will cause the bench to catch fire.

Positioning the Hot Bench

A hot bench must be put in a part of the workshop where the heat will not affect other work, and if large areas of metal are being heated make sure that there is no danger of the ceiling catching fire from the reflected heat. Ideally, the bench should be portable so that it can be moved to the best position when in use and pushed out of the way for the rest of the time. The size and position occupied by the bench will largely depend on the available room in the workshop and the type of work being carried out. Someone making ornamental items will need to use it more than those engaged in general work, who will only want one for occasionally hardening and tempering tools. The watch or jewellery maker will need nothing more than a single brick laid on the bench. Remember heat means subsequent condensation, and this applies particularly when that heat is applied with a gas burner. Condensation in turn means rusty tools, therefore ensure that after carrying out this sort of work tools and machines are wiped free of condensation and sprayed with a light oil.

Also remember that heat can be dangerous and therefore every precaution should be taken to avoid causing a fire. There should always be an extinguisher or fire blanket nearby, in case things go wrong. Safety glasses should be worn when using a blowlamp and thick gloves can protect the hands from burns.

ANNEALING

The aim of heat treatment is either to harden or soften the metal that is being used, and in either case it will involve heating the metal until it changes colour. For example, for steel we want it to go to the colour of a boiled carrot.

Annealing Brass and Copper

If the material to be softened is brass or copper, then there is no need for the slow cooling. Once it has reached the required temperature, it can be dunked in a bucket of water and that will do nicely. Do not heat brass or copper until they are the boiled carrot colour. A dull red will do for either. Nor should they be kept at the temperature for too long – as soon as they reach a dull red, turn the heat off.

Many old textbooks advise getting steel to a cherry red, but this is rather ambiguous as cherries vary in colour. If the steel is to be softened, or annealed, it must be cooled very slowly, so it is best left on the hot bench until cooling is complete. Do not lay it on a concrete floor or anything similar, as the cooling process will be far too rapid and the softening effect lost. The colour should be maintained for several minutes in order to get the best effect and some particularly hard materials may need to be heated two or three times in order to get the required ductability.

Heating Sheet Metal

There is a danger when heating sheet material that the area being heated is too localized, because the blowlamp is kept in the same position for too long. This will cause the sheet to distort in that area and once this has happened the situation cannot be reversed. Therefore it is necessary to keep the heat source moving over the whole of the metal, so that the change of colour that occurs is consistent on the whole sheet. If the reader is intending to use large sheets of annealed metal on a regular basis, it would be best to make up some form of hot bench that is fitted with the type of burner we associate with a domestic cooker in order to spread the heat over a greater area.

Hardening

Most heat treatment will be carried out on bar stock rather than sheet. It is far easier to get a consistent temperature on a bar, and although there will at times be a need for annealing, it is more likely that we will be trying to harden metal in order to make a special tool. The only difference between annealing and hardening a piece of bar is that when hardening metal as soon as it reaches the required colour it has to be quenched and the quicker the quenching is carried out the better. The medium used for quenching depends on the carbon content of the steel. Silver steel with about 0.5 per cent can be quenched in cold water; ground flat stock with 0.9 per cent should be quenched in oil. The reason for the difference is the tendency for the metal to crack with the sudden change of temperature, and the risk of this increases as the carbon content gets higher. It also increases with the area of metal involved, and so if a length of silver steel of over 12mm diameter is to be hardened, that too should be quenched in oil. Mineral oil must not be used under any circumstances. Use a vegetable oil in a reasonable quantity, otherwise it will rapidly heat up and prevent the quick cooling action from occurring. When quenching in oil, there is always a danger of the oil catching fire and suitable precautions to prevent it spreading must be taken. Tools such as punches and

A blowlamp being used to heat a small punch for hardening. Because of its size it is resting on a firebrick instead of being placed on the hot bench.

chisels should only be hardened at the working end; the other end is left soft in order to prevent damage to the hammer used to hit it. Cutting tools such as counter bores, 'D' bits and turning tools must be hardened all over.

Tempering

If a tool remains in its hardened state, it will be too brittle and damage to the cutting edge will occur as soon as it is used. Tempering to prevent this involves cleaning off the black scale that will have been left by the hardening process, until the metal is nice and bright again, then reheating until it discolours, before again quenching it. The cleaning process is done as a rule with emery cloth and is quite time-consuming. Some effort can be saved by coating the metal in soft soap or washing-up liquid prior to heating it for hardening, as the scale is then much more easily removed. Heating for tempering can be done in two ways. In the case of a tool with a soft end, heat can be applied to that end and the changing colour will be seen to run towards the working end – as soon as that end changes to the right colour, quench it. Do not apply excessive heat, as doing so will cause the colours to run too quickly. Not only will it then be difficult to judge the right moment for quenching, but also the varying bands of colour will be too closely spaced. When possible, temper the work

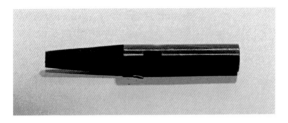

A small taper reamer heated to dark brown for tempering.

completely, rather than allowing the colours to run along it. To do this, the tool should be put either in a small tin of fine sand, for which an old sardine tin is ideal, or laid on a piece of sheet steel. Heat is applied underneath and the changing colours will appear very slowly, giving plenty of control as well as heating the piece through its whole length.

The Colour Sequence

The order in which the colours appear is as follows: light straw; dark straw; light brown; dark brown; purple; dark blue; light blue. Light and dark straw are ideal for lathe cutting tools; light brown for 'D' bits and form tools; purple for chisels; blue for scribers and centre punches; and light blue for springs.

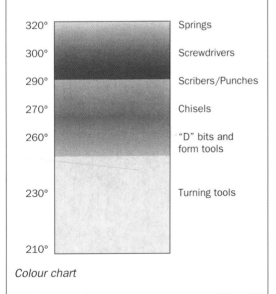

320°	Springs
300°	Screwdrivers
290°	Scribers/Punches
270°	Chisels
260°	"D" bits and form tools
230°	Turning tools
210°	

Colour chart

CASE-HARDENING

Although generally speaking mild steel cannot be hardened and tempered in the same way that high-carbon steel can, it is possible to change the surface structure and obtain a limited depth of hardness, although there is no question of tempering. It is best to use a case-hardening quality steel for the purpose, as it is less effective with the free-cutting varieties that contain lead. The steel is heated to the boiled carrot colour and then immersed in carbon. Specially formulated compounds are sold for the purpose. The steel must be completely covered and the carbon will stick to the surface. It is then reheated until it becomes a bright red colour and the heat maintained for several minutes, after which it is quenched in water. A slightly deeper penetration can be obtained by repeating the process, and finally any carbon remaining on the surface is cleaned off. The depth of the hardness will be quite small, but is sufficient where just a hard surface is required, such as on a bearing surface where it has not been practical to use a high-carbon steel.

SAFETY

It is vital to remember that when heat treatment is being carried out, we are at times dealing with metal that is at a temperature nearing 1,000°C. It goes without saying that a serious burn can result from any misadventure. Also, when metal at such a temperature is plunged into cold water, the surface will rapidly turn to steam and splashes are possible. When quenching in oil there is a danger of the oil catching fire. Should this occur, **never attempt to put it out with water**; instead, exclude the air by placing a piece of metal over the top of the receptacle that is holding the oil. Wear safety glasses at all times and good quality gloves made of leather or cotton; avoid plastic and manmade materials, and if possible make sure that someone is on hand in case of mishaps.

3 Measuring and Marking Out

The metalworker will generally work to much finer tolerances than a woodworker. The latter would expect an accuracy of about 1mm, while the metalworker will be seeking an accuracy of a tenth of that. There are now many devices that help us to achieve this, and although the good old-fashioned tools still have their uses they are now supplemented by more sophisticated equipment. Most work will be carried out by referring to drawings of one sort or another. These might be the metalworker's personal drawings or something published in one of the many magazines that are available, or they might be a full-sized drawings made by a professional draughtsman. With the exception of the first instance, in which case the person concerned will or should be able to understand what he or she has drawn, it will be necessary to be able to decipher a drawing accurately.

A word of warning – draughtsman can and do make mistakes. In a factory, these mistakes are rectified, but drawings that are produced for sale to the public and those published in magazines rarely are. This is no reflection on the people concerned, as it is just plainly impractical to make the necessary corrections, but it does mean that before actually carrying out an operation it is as well to check to see whether a measurement matches that of a mating part. If it does not, establish which is the correct measurement and modify as necessary. This is not likely to be an everyday occurrence, but can happen and there is nothing more annoying than having spent several hours making a part possibly from some fairly expensive material, only to find that through no fault of one's own it is not of any use.

METRIC OR IMPERIAL?

A number of years ago a decision was made by the British Government that the country would convert from the imperial to the metric system of measurement. This has happened in some industries, but at the time of writing has not completely done so in matters of engineering, with the result that it is necessary to have a knowledge of each system. There are many reasons why the changeover has not been completed; for one, it is very difficult to change machinery that is based on working to imperial standards to working to the metric system. Many of the manufacturers of the material we use have rolling mills and other machines suitable only for imperial working, and so although things are now changing, some materials are still only available to imperial standards, while others can be obtained in metric sizes alone. Another major factor is our relationship with the USA, where there is no intention of converting to the metric system.

One thing that should be borne in mind is that it is very difficult, if not absolutely impossible, to make a project using both systems. Other than where threads are concerned, in all other aspects it is advisable to use a single system only.

Each system has its advantages and disadvantages, as well as its devotees. As metalworking generally involves decimal calculations, whichever is chosen the method of calculation will be similar. One fact that readers might find very strange is that in engineering the only metric unit used is the millimetre – centimetres and metres are never referred to. Therefore a measurement of 28cm will be shown on a drawing as 280mm. This same consistency does not apply to imperial work, where both feet and inches are used, and in addition sometimes parts of an inch will be specified in the form of a fraction rather than as a decimal. Instead, therefore of ordering metal 0.5in square it would be referred to as $\frac{1}{2}$in square. Frequently, imperial drawings show work in fraction form, except where particularly fine tolerances are needed.

READING WORKSHOP DRAWINGS

Drawings are generally two-dimensional, with each component drawn to show a different view, so we might see a top, side and end view, or if there was extra detail on one side and it needed further clarification there might be two side views plus the top and end. These views are called projections and there two basic forms, first angle and third angle. As a rough guide, it can be said that first angle is the normal procedure for drawings made in Britain and third angle for those made in the United States. This is not, however, a hard and fast rule, as frequently the person responsible for producing a drawing will have his or her own way of going about things and it is not unknown for third-angle projection to be used in Britain. It all sounds complicated but is really fairly simple. If we take a side view first and rotate it once to right, the second view is said to be in first-angle projection, because the object has been turned once only. If we were to turn it three times and show that view, then it becomes a third-angle projection, and no doubt readers will already have realized that turning it three times to the right is equal to turning it once to the left anyway, the difference being that it is shown on the right of the original component. Don't get too confused and worried about it as the drawings will usually state which angle the projection is so it is easy enough to follow.

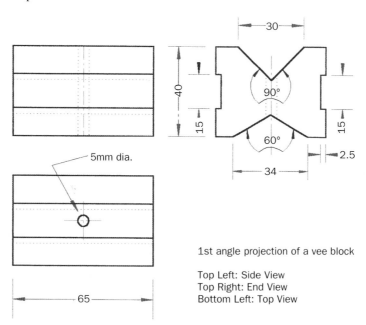

1st angle projection of a vee block

Top Left: Side View
Top Right: End View
Bottom Left: Top View

A first-angle projection of a standard vee block with a hole through the centre.

Lines

The type of line that is used shows a large proportion of the information in drawings. The heavier continuous one shows the outline of the component, while thinner ones are used for dimensioning. Centre lines are lines that, as implied, go either through the centre of the component or through the centre of holes and are shown as dashes and dots and lines; hidden details are always dotted. In addition to this there are lines known as leaders that come either directly from, or after, a small gap from a point on the component, to indicate the points from which a measurement is taken. The measurement lines finish at these leaders with arrows. Providing sufficient room is available, the measuring line will run parallel with the line it indicates and the figures are shown in the centre of it. Sometimes these will be placed in a gap left for the purpose, at other times they will sit on the line itself; which method is used depends on where the draughtsman received his or her training. If there is insufficient room for the measurements to be indicated in this way the indicating arrows may be shown on the outside of the line. Radii are shown by a leader usually with a single arrow, although occasionally on a very large radius the

draughtsman may put two for the purposes of clarification.

Threads

The conventions used to show threads can be confusing to someone who is not well versed in reading drawings, as there are several methods used. The most common is probably a double line, the inner often being in the form of a dash, with a short angular line joining the two at the end. Another convention is a series of short and long lines that theoretically should be drawn at the pitch of the thread, but in practice this rarely happens, the lines just being evenly spaced at no particular distance. Where a drawing is sectioned yet another method is also used, consisting of angled lines, representing the grooves of the thread. Sometimes these might be joined in such a way as to simulate the whole thread, depending on the point of sectioning.

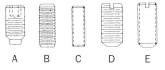

Methods of drawing threads

A: Hexagon Grub screw
B & C: Short Studs
D & E: Slotted Grub Screws

A method of showing threads.

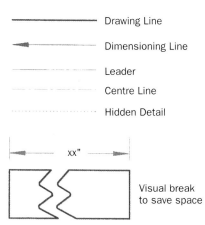

Drawing Line

Dimensioning Line

Leader

Centre Line

Hidden Detail

xx"

Visual break
to save space

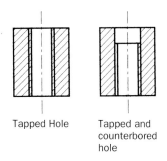

Tapped Hole

Tapped and
counterbored
hole

Types of line likely to be found in engineering drawings.

A second method of illustrating a thread.

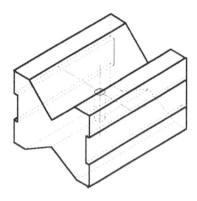

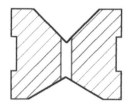

Section at maximum diameter
of hole in vee block

A standard vee block with a hole through the centre shown in isometric projection.

A standard vee block with a hole in the centre shown in section across the central hole.

Isometric Drawing

Occasionally a draughtsman will use a form of drawing known as isometric. This involves drawing all horizontal lines at an angle of 30 degrees and vertical ones as before at 90 degrees; any lines at right angles to those at 30 degrees are set at an angle of 60 degrees, with the resulting drawing being a kind of three-dimensional one. The reasons for its use appear in the first instance to be contradictory, as it is useful for very simple objects where little detail is involved and equally useful for very complicated pieces when it can be difficult to decipher the normal views. This often happens when there are curved surfaces involved together with flat planes and recesses.

Oblique Drawing

Although not very common these days, another form of drawing similar to isometric is known as oblique. Vertical lines are again at 90 degrees, with horizontal ones at zero and intermediates at 45 degrees. It sounds rather complicated, but when viewed is quite straightforward and in certain circumstances very effective. It is more likely to be found in drawings reproduced in magazines.

Sectioning

There are times when it can become very difficult to work out exactly what a drawing represents, particularly if either the outer or inner parts have a number of planes. In these cases, it is normal to show sections of the component. These are represented with a series of diagonal lines and a line marked with letters often shows the point at which the drawing is sectionalized. The sectioned view will therefore be shown as section at A A or B B or something similar, allowing the person reading the drawing to know the exact position that is shown. It is not always the case, and where drawings are published in magazines and space is at a premium, a sectionalized drawing will frequently be shown without any other views. The diagonal lines on a sectioned drawing can be at any angle and often several angles and spacings will be used, to represent either different processes in manufacture or different components that are fitted together.

MEASURING TOOLS

Measuring Instruments

The ruler will be familiar to everyone and still forms the basis of all measuring equipment. Used in conjunction with a pair of dividers it can be a remarkably accurate instrument, and when buying one it is worthwhile investing in a really good one. Only a metal ruler will do, and it is vital that the ruler has good fine markings

A steel rule held in a home-made holder, being used in conjunction with a scriber set in a surface gauge to mark a length of copper tube.

that are as narrow as possible but deep enough to accept a scriber. It is no good buying a ruler with markings that are a 0.25mm wide, because if a measurement was taken between two using the outer edge of each the error could mean 0.5mm.

The Engineer's Square

As with a ruler, a good square should be invested in and it must be treated with every possible care, as it is essential that it is maintained in good condition. It is a good idea to make a small box to keep the square in to prevent it getting damaged. Squares can be obtained in a range of sizes and it is worth having two sizes if possible. Variations on the ordinary engineer's square designed to work at any desired angle, some very sophisticated and working on a vernier system, are unlikely to be

required by the average hobby metalworker, but these do have their uses in their basic form. It is also worth mentioning the protractor, which works in a similar fashion to a square, except that one sets the protractor to the desired angle prior to using it.

The Micrometer

Designed for very fine measurement, the micrometer is a tool that in recent years has seen many developments. It is based on the principal of a screw thread and is best explained in the following way. If we have a screwed plate, the thread having a pitch of 0.5mm, and put a matching screw in it, we know that if a point marked on the plate is compared to a similar one on the thread, every rotation of the screw will have moved it 0.5mm, either up or down, depending on the way it was turned. Two revolutions equals 1mm. Fit a collar marked with fifty divisions and use it to rotate the screw as would a nut, and each time one of those divisions is adjacent to the mark on the plate,

Above *Having been used to mark out, the square is in this case also being used to set the work accurately.*

Left *An adjustable bevel, used in the same way as a square, except that it is set to an angle. This tool is easily made in the workshop.*

A combination set contains a rule with three removable attachments, allowing any desired angle to be measured or marked off.

the thread will have moved one hundredth of a millimetre. As not everyone is able to decipher these marks with their naked eye, some manufacturers placed small magnifying widows

on the tool. The latest device to aid readability is a digital read-out. Instead of us using the thread movement to get the measurement, a tiny electronic sensor does it for us and the measurement shows up in figures on a scale. On the more sophisticated versions there is also a switch to allow one to translate between metric and imperial measurements. Reading an imperial micrometer follows a similar pattern.

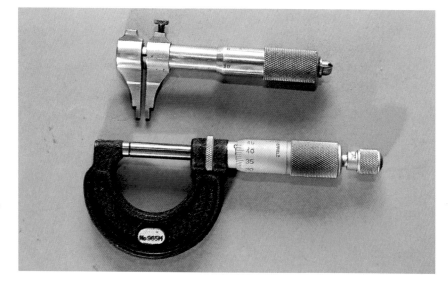

Two micrometers: the top one is for measuring internally, such as cylinder bores; the lower is a standard 25mm metric micrometer.

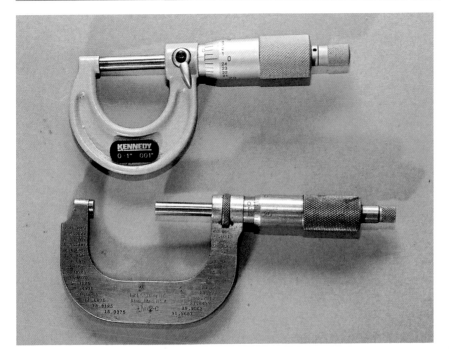

Left *Imperial 1in and 2in micrometers.*

Below *It is a good idea to make a simple stand such as this to hold the micrometer. It helps to protect it from damage, stops it getting mislaid and many items can be measured while it is on the stand, giving it a nice steady position.*

Reading an Imperial Micrometer

Readings are taken from a combination of sleeve and thimble, the lower edge of the latter is bevelled and divided into twenty five parts, each of which represent a thousandth of an inch. There is a datum line on the sleeve and this is divided into numbered divisions of tenths of an inch and each of these divisions is divided into four that measure twenty five thousandths. The mark on the sleeve is read and the marking on the thimble used to measure the difference between any two divisions on the sleeve. In the drawing the marks on the sleeve are at four tenths plus three complete divisions of twenty five thousandths, the thimble marking shows that a further ten thousandths of an inch need to be added, giving a total reading of 0.045".

Reading a Metric Micrometer

In this case the thimble is divided into fifty parts and the sleeve into millimetres, with markings at every five marked above the datum line. Half millimetre divisions are shown below the line, as with the Imperial Micrometer the main reading is taken from the sleeve and those on the thimble will divide them by fifty. The drawing shows ten millimetres above the datum and a half below, plus another fifteen divisions that are to be added. One turn of the thimble moves it half a millimetre so as it has fifty divisions the movement between each must be one hundredth of a millimetre. The drawing shows the thimble just past the ten millimetre mark and the sleeve at sixteen, the reading therefore is ten millimetres and sixteen one hundredths or 10.16mm.

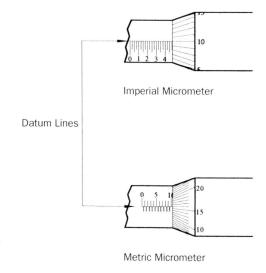

Imperial Micrometer

Datum Lines

Metric Micrometer

Reading micrometers.

Vernier Calipers

The vernier caliper takes care of larger sizes, and although the most common size is 150mm (6in), they are made in much longer lengths. Most calipers have the ability to measure in three ways – outside, inside and length. It is possible to read a measurement on a vernier scale to two-hundredths of a millimetre or one-thousandth of an inch. The system used relies on the fact that divisions on the vernier scale are minutely smaller than those on the main scale, and by balancing the two scales it is possible to read parts of the divisions.

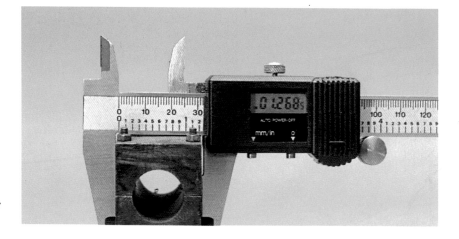

A digital type of vernier gauge that reads both metric and imperial and converts either at the touch of a button.

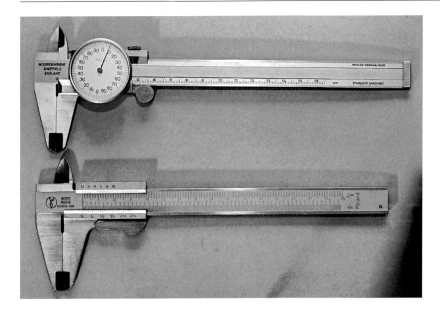

Two types of vernier gauge: the top has a dial to make reading the small measurements easier; the lower is a standard type that reads both metric and imperial.

Measurement of inside diameters

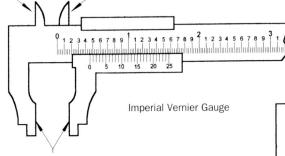

Imperial Vernier Gauge

Measurement of outside diameters

Reading a Imperial Vernier Gauge

The measurements on the body of an imperial vernier are in inches and sub divided into tenths. The lower scale is marked with twenty five divisions. To read it take the nearest division on the body to the zero on the moving section, then look along the sliding scale to see which division lines up exactly with one on the body, that reading is added to the original one from the body. The drawing shows the zero at about or just over halfway between four and five, the number on the sliding scale that lines up exactly with one at the top is twenty, so the reading is four tenths of an inch plus twenty one thousandths or 0.420. Note the small lines on the fixed scale are only there as marks with which to line up the moving scale, a common mistake is to try and interpret these as a reading when they are in fact graduation marks, pure and simple.

Reading vernier scales.

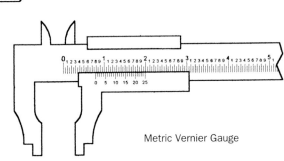

Metric Vernier Gauge

Reading a Metric Vernier Gauge

The fixed scale on a metric vernier in half millimetres with every tenth millimetre numbered as one – two – thee, etc. The sliding scale is divided into twenty five parts, or on very expensive instruments fifty parts. As with the imperial instrument take the nearest figure on the fixed scale to zero the sliding scale and then find the line on the sliding scale that coincides with a fixed one. The number on the sliding scale is added to the figure on the fixed scale to give the final result. The drawing shows zero at just past seven and a half millimetres, the line on the sliding scale that coincides with a fixed one is fifteen so the reading is 7.65mm.

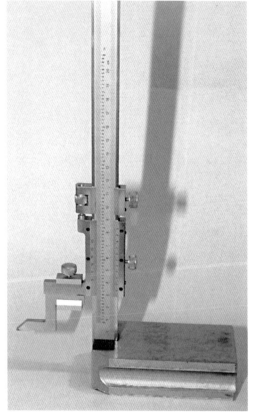

Right *A vernier height gauge. Used for marking out, it has a solid base that can be slid along a smooth flat surface and the pointer is hardened.*

Above *A vernier height gauge in use. Both components can be marked at the same height with the sure knowledge that there will be no discrepancy between the two.*

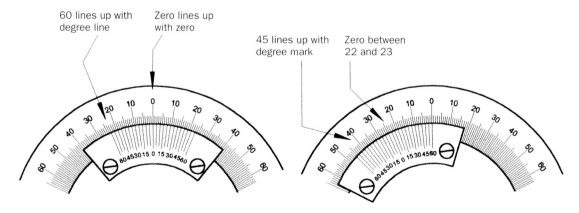

The main scale is graduated in degrees of a circle but marked off in units of ten from either side of Zero, thus creating two semi circles of 180°. The Vernier Scale has 12 divisions each side of zero, each division therefore equals $\frac{1}{12}$ of 60, which is 5 minutes of arc. These divisions occupy the same space as 23 divisions on the main scale with the result that the reading is taken as the nearest whole degree on the main scale plus the reading on the Vernier Scale in line with a main scale division.

The reading on the left is zero, the one on the right 22° 45 minutes.

Scales for Vernier Protractors

DIAL GAUGES

The dial gauge is more commonly known as a clock gauge, or sometimes it is just plainly called a clock. These instruments are used for setting work on machines and are capable of reading to a similar accuracy as a micrometer.

More often than not they will be held in special clamps to the machine by a magnet, movable arms allowing for adjustment. Clock gauges are available for metric or imperial readings, although with some of the more sophisticated versions it is possible to read either form.

A clock gauge in use when setting work accurately on a milling machine.

Magnetic holders, etc. that are used to set a clock gauge into position. The holders have an arrangement of flexible arms to allow for maximum adjustment.

Depth Gauges

Vernier calipers have a built-in depth gauge, but it might not prove practical to use this, possibly because using the in-built one involves standing the tool on end, and the end as a rule does not provide a very good platform from which to obtain a measurement. Most people therefore prefer the simple task of making a depth gauge for themselves, which consists of a bar of rectangular metal with a hole through which is pushed a rod that acts as a probe and is secured with a knurled screw. The probe is pushed into the recess to be measured and locked with the screw; it is then measured with an ordinary ruler. Depth micrometers can also be purchased if there is a regular need to measure depths accurately. However, it is fair to say that these are rarely used, the use of a ruler being adequate for the measuring of most holes.

A different use for the depth gauge. By measuring the component in the vice in several different places it was possible to establish that it was truly level.

Two home-made depth gauges. The one on the left is a standard type. On the right is a spring-loaded one. It was made that way because the probe is only 1mm in diameter in order to measure some tiny components and because of their size it was not be practical to tighten a screw.

MARKING-OUT TOOLS

Using Marking-Out Fluids

The marking out of metal mainly involves scratching lines on the surface and making small indentations at various places. These indentations serve two purposes – they make it easier to see the position of a line, and can also act as a guide for drilling holes. It is normal practice to cover the surface of the metal with some sort of dye. The instrument used to make the line cuts through the dye, leaving a bright line. The liquid sold especially for marking out is usually spirit-based and coloured blue, although other colours are available. It can be bought in the form of an aerosol spray, or as a liquid to be applied with a brush. Before it is applied by either method it is essential to ensure that the surface of the metal is completely free of grease and oil. Wiping it over with methylated spirit or washing it with a strong solution of washing-up liquid can achieve this.

There are a number of tools that have stood the test of time that are also used for both measuring and marking out. Used many centuries ago and yet still just as valuable to the engineer today are dividers and calipers. Together with their first cousin, odd-leg calipers that are frequently called Jennies,

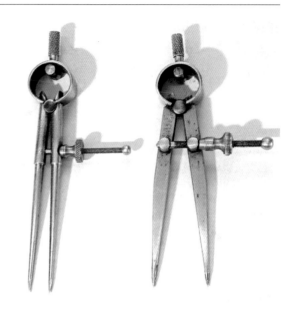

Two types of divider, although both do the same job. Although as their appearance suggests they are useful for scribing arcs and circles, they are also a means of measuring length very accurately. The points are located in the divisions of a rule and the measurement can be transferred to the work.

calipers are particularly valuable for scribing lines parallel with an edge.

The centre punch is another valuable tool. The name centre punch is often used to

---

Alternate Marking-Out Media

Copper Sulphate

An old-fashioned medium used as a marking fluid is a solution of copper sulphate, consisting of a dessertspoon or thereabouts of crystals dissolved in a jam jar full of water and applied with a brush. To use this, the metal needs to be very clean indeed, and as well as wiping it with a degreasing liquid, it is necessary to rub it over with a piece of fine emery paper or cloth. The metal takes on a bright copper colour after it has been applied and scratch marks show through it as a bright silver colour. The result is much more permanent than marking-out fluid, which easily chips off and will rub away if it comes into contact with a number of different liquids.

Emulsion Paint

The application of ordinary emulsion paint can make an excellent marking fluid through which marks will show up very clearly. The paint needs to be thinned with water before use and must not be applied too thickly for it to work properly.

Felt-Tip Pen

Where only a small area is involved, using a felt-tip pen can be a good idea. Some pens are sold that are designed especially to be applied to metal surfaces.

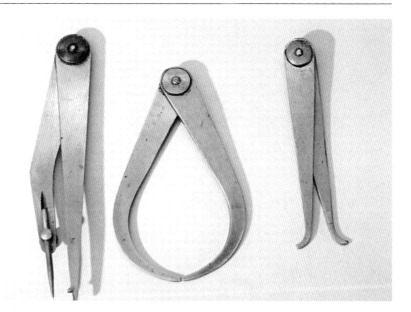

*Three types of
calipers: left, odd-leg;
centre, outside;
right, inside.*

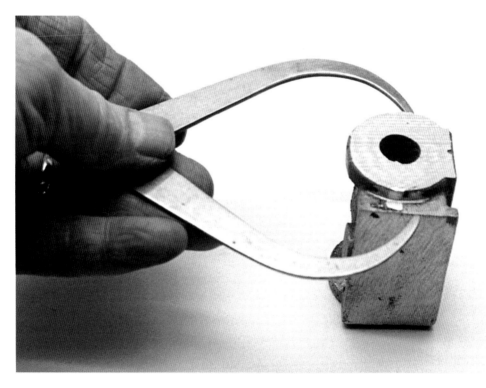

*Outside calipers being use to check the
measurement of an awkward casting. They are
pulled across what is required to be measured,
until they slide through with the tiniest bit of*

*friction and the distance between the jaw ends is
measured. A similar process would be used to
measure the bore of the hole with inside calipers.*

The caliper leg of the Jennie is rested against the edge of the work and the tool drawn along; the scriber leaves a line parallel to the edge of the piece. The Jennies works equally well on a radius and are a very valuable and efficient tool.

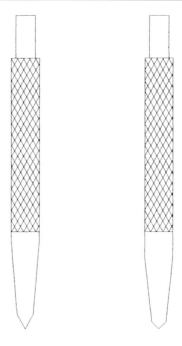

Left, a dot punch; right, a centre punch. Although very similar in appearance and more often than not both are referred to as centre punches, the two tools have different purposes. The dot punch has a point at 60 degrees that allows one to feel a scribed line. The centre punch is located in the indentation left by the dot punch and the 90-degree angle is convenient for locating a centre drill or drill.

describe all types of centre punch, but there are in fact two distinct forms: the dot punch, which has a point angle of 60 degrees; and the centre punch, which has a point angle of 90 degrees. The dot punch is used for the initial marking of a point, while the centre punch is used for marking the position where a hole is to be drilled, the 90-degree angle allowing a drill to settle into the indentation it has made. It is possible to buy automatic centre punches, which have a button on the top; when pressed, a spring is released and the punch gives a sharp forward tap, thus avoiding the use of a hammer and also leaving one hand free to support the work.

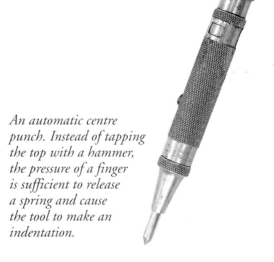

An automatic centre punch. Instead of tapping the top with a hammer, the pressure of a finger is sufficient to release a spring and cause the tool to make an indentation.

The automatic centre punch being operated; the internal spring is adjustable giving differing pressures for use on different metals.

Another important tool is the scriber. These are manufactured in a variety of sizes and have a point at an angle of 60 degrees. They are used for marking lines.

Measure Twice, Scribe Once

A scriber should only be drawn along once in a single movement. Drawing it along more than that will almost inevitably result in a double line, and no matter how minute the distance between the two, there is the potential for a build-up of errors. The same applies when scribing arcs and circles; one movement only should be made. It is better by far to double or treble check a measurement before making the mark, rather than go ahead and then have to try to correct it afterwards.

Scribers are available in all shapes and sizes and can easily be made in the workshop in order to get one that feels right for the individual. The one in the photograph is rather unusual, as it has a weighted ball on the top that is sprung-loaded, rather like the automatic centre punch. The point, which is at 60 degrees, is used to scribe a line, and without taking it off the work, the punch is released, leaving an indentation in the line. The result is more accurate than using a scriber and separate punch.

A surface plate is used to ensure accuracy when marking out. This consists of a ground cast-iron block that is made to a very high standard and can be relied upon to be perfectly flat and accurate. At one time they were made by craftsmen who scraped the surface by hand, but nowadays it is far more likely that they will have been ground flat. Care must be taken to ensure that the surface is maintained.

A good alternative to a surface block is a piece of plate glass at least 12mm (0.5in) thick, with the edges ground smooth, plate glass being

Above *A surface plate is an aid to accurate marking out and is seen here with a pair of vee blocks, which are used to support round objects and parallels that are specially ground steel bars used to support work.*

Left *When not in use the surface plate should be protected and here we see one with a wooden cover that has been made for that purpose.*

Above *Greater accuracy can be achieved if the work is clamped vertically and lines scribed with a surface gauge or vernier height gauge.*

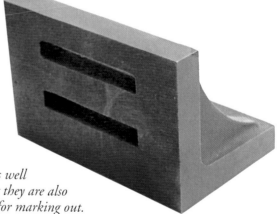

Right *Angle plates like this have many uses. As well as using them for clamping work for machining they are also useful for ensuring that items are at 90 degrees for marking out.*

manufactured to a particularly high standard. It may well be possible to obtain an off-cut of a suitable size from a glazier.

Using a Datum

When a number of marks need to be made at intervals along a line, whether it be for other dissecting lines or for punch marks, never measure from one to the other. For example, if the first position to be marked is at 20mm from the end of the work and the second one another 20mm and the third, say, yet another 20mm,

do not measure from the first to the second and the second to the third, as doing this will build up errors. Suppose, for example, we have a piece of work that requires ten intersections on a line all at 20mm intervals. If when measuring the first mark, an error of one-tenth of a millimetre is made, and such an error when using a ruler is not beyond the bounds of possibility, then a measurement is taken from the second mark to the third and a similar error occurs and this continues right through the ten intersection, by the time the last one is reached the overall error has gone from one tenth to a whole millimetre, which is definitely an unacceptable error. It is a situation that is particularly likely to arise in these circumstances, as once the dividers have been set to get the measurement it is unlikely any change will be made.

Suppose, however, that a different approach is made to marking out. We still get that tenth of a millimetre error on the first intersection, but if the next intersection is measured from the same end as the first one and the tenth of a

Surface gauges or scribing blocks. The one on the left is a simple project made in the workshop, the one on the right a commercial product.

millimetre error again occurs, then instead of the second mark having an error of two-tenths, it is still only one. Assuming that for some reason we continue to make that same error every time a measurement is taken, then when we come to the last intersection the error is still one-tenth rather than a whole millimetre, which is much more acceptable.

Points where holes are to be drilled should be lightly dot-punched first, then a centre punch used to make the final mark, locating it centrally in the mark made by the dot punch. It is also a very good idea to lightly dot-punch at regular intervals along a line that is to be used for cutting, as marking fluids can become very faint or rub off altogether; if tiny dot punch

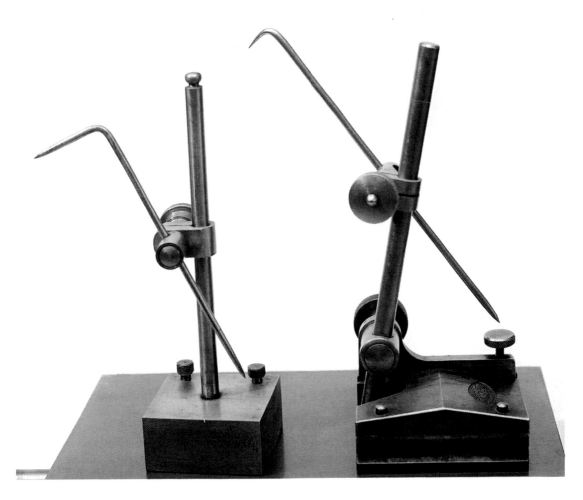

The parts of a home-made surface gauge.

marks are made these can be seen even when the original line cannot. When marking out flat plate, far greater accuracy can be achieved if the work is stood on edge and clamped to an angle plate, on a known flat surface. Horizontal lines can be scribed with a height gauge, the scriber of which has been set to the required measurement.

Decorative Ironwork

Usually people wishing to make decorative ironwork need a slightly different marking-out technique, as they will be using black mild steel and the bending and twisting of the metal will be the order of the day. No marking-out medium will be required, but otherwise normal practice is needed when it comes to cutting and drilling marks. The latter should be punched quite deeply and if possible a start on the holes made with a centre drill, as during the sort of processes involved with this work, fine punch marks will quickly disappear. Where the metal is to be bent or twisted, all marking out should be done with finely pointed chalk; this also

applies to any places where welding is to be carried out.

Working on Round Material

So far, consideration has only been given to marking out flat surfaces, but from time to time it will be necessary to mark on round bar. Although the same tools and methods will be used, supporting the metal calls for something different. To just mark out a centre, it is quite permissible to hold the work in a vice and use either odd-leg calipers or a centre gauge, where it will be necessary to mark the end. For something more complicated, perhaps to establish cutting lines, or possibly points where a number of holes will be needed, trying to stand the bar on end and mark the top of it will not work as there will be insufficient support. In most cases, the work should be supported on a vee block, or two matching blocks if it is a long piece. Marking out can then be done with a height gauge, or, if one of those is not available, a scribing block, with the scriber point set to height by reference to a ruler in

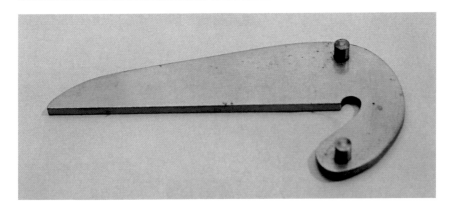

Above *A centre gauge. The two pins are equidistant from the straight edge and when laid on the end of a round bar with them facing down, the edge is lined exactly along the centre. Once again, the tool is a simple one that can be made in the workshop.*

Below *A round bar supported on vee blocks and marked with the scriber of a surface gauge.*

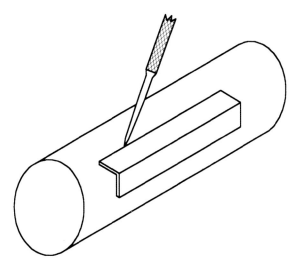

A length of angle can be used to scribe a line lengthways along a round bar or tube.

a stand. Trying to work with an unsupported tool will mean a loss of accuracy, so it is essential that both the work and tools be well supported.

To mark out lengthways on a round bar, it must again be properly supported and in this case it is best to use an angle plate and secure the bar to it. A toolmaker's clamp is the ideal thing to use, but sometimes this may not be practical as the clamp itself is likely to get in the way. A different approach will then have to be tried, as once marking out has commenced the work must not be moved at all. One way of securing it is to stick it to an angle plate with double-sided adhesive tape. Another way is to work on either the drilling table or a milling machine table and hold the bar with clamps fitted in the tee slots.

It is no use trying to hold a ruler to the bar in order to mark lines along its length, as it will inevitably slip. Scribing marks should be made using either a scribing block or a height gauge. If a scribing block is used, the scriber must be firmly secured and the end being used kept as short as possible – the longer the overlap, the greater the torque at the end and therefore the greater the chance that the scriber will move from its initial setting. If for any reason it is not practical to use either of these, instead of trying to scribe the line along a rule use a piece of angle iron, as this will sit nicely on the bar and can be retained by hand or with adhesive tape.

4 Cutting, Filing and Finishing

CUTTING

Possibly the most basic need that the home metalworker will have is to cut metal in the form of sheet or bar either by hand or by mechanical means. Even if some mechanical assistance in the form of powered equipment might be available, it is inevitable that at some time or another the work will have to be carried out by hand, as there are very few workshops other than those in professional engineering companies that could justify the cost or the workshop space to install the heavy machinery required for all types of metal cutting.

Hacksawing

Generally speaking, cutting pieces off a length of bar appears to need little description, but there are two basic rules that must be followed at all times. The first is always to support the work as near to the cut as possible, and the second is never to hurry, as doing so will only result in disaster. All cutting tools are designed

Lubrication

The use of a small drop of cutting oil will help when cutting mild steel and a drop of white spirit or paraffin can be of assistance when cutting copper or brass. It should not be used if the copper is subsequently to be hard soldered, as it is impossible to remove completely and this will result in failure of the joint. Under no circumstances should any form of lubrication be used when sawing cast iron.

to work at a specific speed and when we deal with the lathe, drilling and milling machines this will again be stressed. Often one is trying to get what can be a bit of an irksome task out of the way quickly, and so the hacksaw tends to be moved at a rapid pace in short strokes across the metal, but this only results in blunt tools and inaccurate cutting. In effect, the central part of the hacksaw blade is being rapidly worn away, and so the amount of actual cutting it does gets less and less with every movement. In addition, the heat generated when working like this adds towards blunting the hacksaw, whereas with a longer stroke there is more opportunity for it to cool down. Most metals will harden to some degree as work is carried out on them; if the sawing is done too quickly the hardening effect increases, causing even greater wear on the teeth.

Most people who have not been told otherwise tend to work with all these faults, believing that the quicker the blade is moved the sooner the metal will be cut through, whereas in fact it has exactly the opposite effect.

Keep the Cut Straight

A hacksaw is one of those tools that appears to have a mind of its own, with a seemingly inbuilt ability to cut at angles instead of straight lines. The slower-paced long stroke will go some way towards obviating this, but it can still be useful to have some sort of guide to work to. This in most cases consists of a scribed line, but as cutting proceeds the line can become much harder to see, the result of a build-up of a burr

Masking tape round a length of large diameter tubing to act as a guide when sawing; it can equally be used as a guide on flat surfaces.

It can be seen from the photograph that the saw has been guided through the work perfectly straight as a result of the tape guide.

as well as dust that tends to congeal along the edge of the cut, making it difficult to see the line. A good idea is to put a strip of masking tape along the line that is being worked to, as the tape will be visible when the line would not.

Hacksaw Frames

Most people will be familiar with a hacksaw frame. There are various shapes and the choice of which type is considered most suitable is purely personal. Some people like to have a handle that runs in line with the blade, while others prefer it at 90 degrees. Most frames have a screw fitting at one end for blade adjustment, with a fixed fitting at the opposite end; a few have a cam action instead of a screw. It will be

as well to have a good look around to see which type will be best suited to the individual. Similar to the hacksaw, but as the name implies much smaller, is the junior hacksaw, and here again there is wide variety in the types of frames and once again it is a matter of personal choice.

Wide Cuts

Sometimes it may be necessary to cut a slot using the hacksaw and possibly the blade will not cut quite wide enough to achieve the desired result. With most hacksaw frames it is quite possible to mount two blades side by side and this will increase the width of the cut.

Blade Quality

No matter what type of frame is purchased, the ultimate result will rest on the blade that is fitted to it. The first piece of advice, before going into technicalities, must be do not be tempted to purchase inferior blades as they are a waste of time. Tests carried out between some bought on a market stall, when compared with those of a recognized and old-established manufacturer, showed the better quality blade lasted fifty times as long as the cheaper item. Yet again, a good tool shop is recommended and mostly the staff will be able to offer expert advice on the best blade to use for a particular job. Blades are, or should be, made of hardened metal with teeth that are relieved at the back. The teeth cut only on the forward stroke and dragging them back across the work will only serve to rub away the cutting edge. The first rule of sawing, therefore, which also applies to filing, is to cut only in one direction – do not rub the tool backwards and forwards across the work. It is also necessary to use strokes that are as long as possible.

The metal from which blades are made comes in three forms – carbon steel, high-speed steel and bi-metal, the latter being a mixture of carbon and high-speed steel, cleverly designed so that the teeth made of high-speed steel are supported by a carbon steel back. The merits of different types of steel were discussed in Chapter One and it will no doubt be recalled that high-speed steel is specially designed for the manufacture of cutting tools. It follows that high-speed steel is going to be the most efficient when it comes to cutting metal, but unfortunately it is also much more brittle than carbon steel. Many people without the ability to use a hacksaw correctly tend to find that high-speed blades shatter easily, once again the result of trying to cut too rapidly and in so doing imparting a twist to the blade that causes it to snap. Carbon steel blades, which are often described as flexible blades, therefore became popular as they were better suited to this sort of misuse, particularly in school workshops where youngsters tend to be far too impatient with the

result that a high-speed blade would last only a few minutes. The introduction of the bi-metal blade has to some extent solved this problem, but as the blades are comparatively expensive, carbon steel is still frequently used. As a result, they are still obtainable but readers are advised only to consider the use of bi-metal or high speed. Of the two, the high-speed blade remains the most efficient and if treated properly there will be no problems with broken blades.

Saw Blade Teeth

Hacksaw blades are sold not only with reference to the metal from which they are made, but also with various tooth spacings. At the time of writing, metrication, in Britain at least, has not occurred as far as this is concerned, and they are standardized as fourteen, eighteen, twenty-four and thirty-two teeth per inch, although the fourteen-tooth blade is rarely used. Coarser specifications are used for power hacksaws. Blades for the junior hacksaw are available as thirty-two or fourteen teeth per inch, although only the thirty-two-tooth type is intended for use with metal. The fourteen-tooth blade is

General Use of Hacksaw Blades			
Material	Number of teeth per diameter/thickness		
	Below 2mm	2–5mm	Above 5mm
Mild steel	32	24	18
Carbon steel	32	24	18–24
High-carbon steel	32	24	24
Cast iron	24–32	18–24	18
Copper	24–32	18–24	18
Brass & bronze	24–32	18–24	18
Aluminium	24–32	18–24	18
Hard plastics	24–32	18–24	18

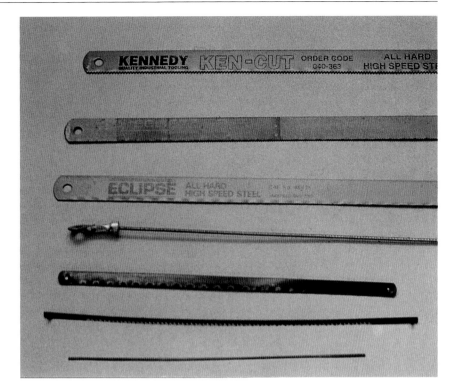

Metal cutting blades of various types. The top three are grades of hacksaw blades, below those a sawing wire, a junior hacksaw blade, a coping and a piercing saw.

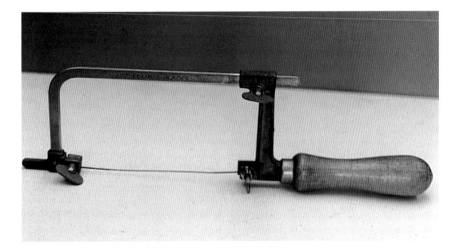

The coping saw is designed for use on wood, but is also ideal for cutting awkward shapes in thin metal.

designed for working with wood, but from time to time the metalworker nowadays finds him or herself using plastic of one type or another and the fourteen-tooth blade can be very useful for that. Either type is only available in carbon steel and the life of the blades tends to be rather limited.

Saws for Cutting Radii

Coping saws are designed for wood, but are very good for cutting intricate shapes in sheet brass. They use only a fourteen-tooth blade, which can be a rather too coarse on very thin sheet. Piercing saws use blades of four different pitches which are identical to those for fret saws; the pitches are sixteen, eighteen, twenty-two and thirty-two and all are made of carbon steel, which gives them plenty of flexibility although they do wear out very quickly. Nevertheless, the coping saw is an excellent tool for cutting thin sheet metal and should find a place in any home workshop.

Radial Hacksaw Blades

To use an ordinary hacksaw to generate curves, a radial hacksaw blade that old-time craftsmen always referred to as a sawing wire is used. It is a length of flexible steel impregnated with tiny pieces of tungsten that fits between the fixing screws of the hacksaw frame. The wire can be used in either direction as there are no teeth as such and so it is drawn back across the work as well as cutting on the forward stoke. This two-way motion is essential, as there is invariably a tendency for the wire to bind when lifted off the cut. The binding is almost certainly caused by a tiny amount of expansion of the metal caused by the heat created when cutting.

Other Types of Hand Saw

There are some circumstances where it is not possible to use a hacksaw in the normal manner, a typical example being if a piece of

---

Blade Reversal

With coping, piercing and pad saws it can be advantageous to reverse the blade. When using a hacksaw the teeth should point forwards, with the other three types a better and more accurate cut can be obtained with them pointing towards the handle. The blade should still be lifted on the return stroke.

---

metal needs to be cut along its length and the length of the cut is greater than the depth of the hacksaw blade. The tool to deal with this is a pad saw, the name given to what amounts to a handle made to accept a hacksaw blade, so there is no restriction behind it and in theory any length can be cut. This means the use of a somewhat shortened blade and in turn that the teeth wear very quickly, but with the saw only being used on thin sheet material it is not too much of a handicap.

A pad saw is designed to accept a normal hacksaw blade but only uses one end of it, because at that end there is no restriction of a frame. Longer lengths can be cut than is the case with a normal hacksaw.

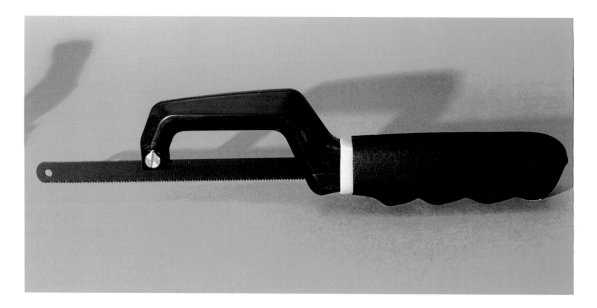

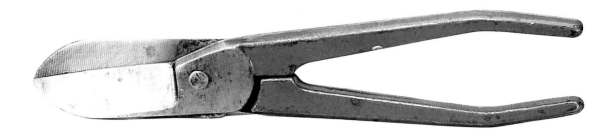

SHEET METAL CUTTING

Hand Shears

Very thin material is the easiest of all to cut. Frequently this can be done with shears, which are usually called tin-snips and can be bought in a variety of sizes. 1.5mm brass and 1mm steel are about the maximum anyone will be able to cut using these, and even then a fairly large pair will be required and quite a lot of strength. In general therefore, the use of hand shears should be confined to much thinner metals and for this purpose they are capable of cutting quite complex shapes. Of course, there always seems to be a downside and in this case it is the distortion that the shears can make. They tend to bend the metal at the edges and although in most instances it is quite easy to push it back into shape, doing so can create unsightly marks that cannot always be removed. When cutting curves it is therefore advisable to cut a series of straight lines, gradually removing smaller pieces of metal and finishing off with a file.

Bench Shears

An advance on the hand shear is the type used on the bench. These too come in a variety of sizes and a large one will usually deal with brass up to a thickness of 2mm and mild steel to 1.5mm. Although designed to be screwed to a bench, because there is more often than not a lack of bench space in the home workshop they are frequently bolted to a block of hardwood, which is held in the vice, thereby allowing the shear to be put away when not required. Like

Metal cutting shears (tin-snips), useful for cutting thin sheet metal.

the hand shear, they will cut accurately and do a certain amount of shaping as well. Also as when using the hand shear, for generating curves it is best to cut a series of straight lines and remove any surplus with a file. They create less distortion than the hand shear and the blades are capable of being removed for sharpening, which means that they can be taken to a company specializing in such work for grinding.

Rollers and Nibblers

A more unusual but quite effective device for cutting sheet metal consists of a roller cutting blade, which when rotated removes a thin sliver of the material, leaving a fairly clean edge either side of the cut. This allows quite a degree of flexibility when cutting radii. A similar system is used with a tool known as a nibbler. These can be hand or power operated, the hand type operating in a similar fashion to the rotary tool described above by cutting a thin strip of metal and leaving a clean cut on either side. All these tools are only useful for thin sheet metal up to about 1.5mm thick brass and 1.2mm steel. Power nibblers are available as complete machines or an adaption for a normal hand-held-drill. They work on an entirely different principle to the other types already mentioned, punching a series of square holes along the metal that are so closely spaced as to form a continuous cut, which is very clean indeed. The tools are quick to use, but the continuous

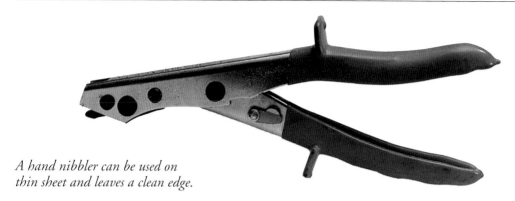

*A hand nibbler can be used on
thin sheet and leaves a clean edge.*

punching action creates a great deal of noise, and effective as they may be, because of the noise they may not be suitable when a workshop is adjacent to housing. The self-contained nibbler, which is even noisier, is capable of cutting thicker material than the type that is made as an attachment for a drill; the latter usually will cope with steel to a thickness of about 1.5mm and a large one with a thickness of 3.5mm. The operating mechanism of any nibbler must be kept well oiled and cutting lubricant is advisable when used on mild steel.

Power Saws

As well as the hand-held saws there are several types of power saws that can be used to save a lot of manual work. For example, a good quality DIY type of jigsaw fitted with a suitable blade can be useful when cutting sheet metal up to a thickness of about 3mm, and it will cut radii as well as straight lines. It is not the easiest of tools to use on metal when hand-held, but can be very efficient if screwed underneath a wooden base and then clamped in a vice, so that it is used upside down. For best results, an orbital or pendulum action saw is needed as

An ordinary DIY jigsaw fitted upside down to a bench can make a very good power saw, capable of cutting shapes as well as straight. It is essential to fit a retaining bar to prevent too much vibration.

this takes the blade away from the work on the return stroke. There are numerous types of blades for metal cutting available. They are usually designed for specific materials and with the right blade the saw will be capable of cutting quite thick material. Once again, do not be tempted to buy the blades at the DIY shop, as of necessity these places stock only tools designed for general purposes and they are not really suitable for the dedicated metalworker.

Bandsaws

Bandsaws are available as two- or three-wheel types, and in a large variety of sizes. In general, it is fair to say that the two-wheel type is more suited to metalworking than those with three wheels, if only because it is easier to set up. However, the throat of the three-wheeled version will be wider than the two-wheel type,

allowing a bigger area of metal to pass underneath. Although most that are sold for DIY purposes are advertised as capable of metal cutting, frequently they will only cut very thin sheet and often the blades sold for metal cutting are of inferior quality and the teeth wear away very quickly. The remedy is to find a Saw Doctor (their details are to be found in *Yellow Pages*) and have blades fashioned to the correct size for the machine. No matter how good the blade, the machine must be capable of running at or near the correct speed, which will depend to some extent on the diameter of the wheels. As a rough guide, we require a driving pulley speed of around one hundred revolutions a minute.

Very popular are vertical/horizontal bandsaws designed especially for metalwork. They are used horizontally for cutting heavy bar and also vertically as a bandsaw. The blades

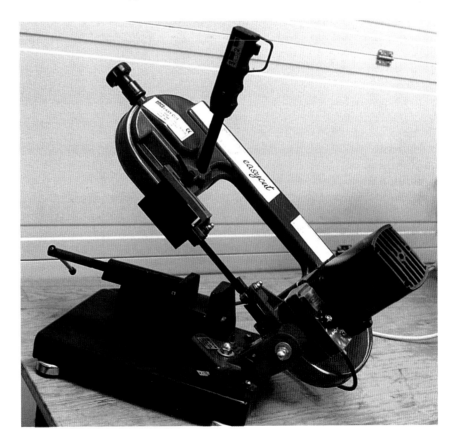

A portable bandsaw that is fitted with a tungsten blade and capable of cutting through thick bar stock.

are generally much broader than those found on saws designed to be used in the vertical position only. This has the disadvantage that it is not possible to cut small radii with them. The traditional power saw of the reciprocating type that replicates the action of a hacksaw is available freely on the second-hand market, and is often made as a project in the home workshop. Castings are available from suppliers of model engineering equipment, although many people build them from basic materials. Home-made ones often use an ordinary hacksaw blade rather than the special heavy blades used with the commercial types; some use half a blade, giving greater stability. With all power-saw work it is advisable to use a cutting fluid when possible, although this should not be done when working on cast iron.

Slitting Saws

A slitting saw is a very thin, circular blade of small diameter, which is held on an arbor and used either in the lathe or the milling machine. Because of this, it is possible to adjust the machine setting and obtain absolute accuracy. Using a fine feed the finished edge will be far better than the results obtained with any other type of saw. The length and depth of cut is limited by the travel of the machine and the diameter of the saw. Speeds and feeds should be appropriate for the metal used – any attempt to rotate the saw too fast or to feed into the metal too fast will result in so much heat being generated that the saw will be rendered useless in no time at all.

FILING AND FINISHING

Filing appears to be a simple, straightforward process, but like so many metalworking operations is not quite as simple as it at first appears. This is reflected in the fact that when there were craft apprenticeships, many weeks would be spent by the apprentice, filing and sawing until the necessary state of perfection was reached. The craftsman would be expected to be able to file accurately to within a

A slitting saw being used in a milling machine to slice through a casting.

thousandth part of an inch or one hundredth of a millimetre.

Filing Techniques

The technique required for filing is remarkably similar to that needed for using a hacksaw and like a hacksaw the teeth cut only on the forward stroke; dragging it back across the work will only serve to wear down the cutting edge. So the first rule of filing, as with sawing, is to cut only in one direction – the file must not rub backwards and forwards across the work and use strokes as long as possible. The same applies to the speed at which the tool is used; if the work is done too quickly the metal will harden, causing extra wear on the teeth.

The file should, for normal work, be kept as flat as possible and unless an angle is required, maintained at 90 degrees to the work. Before commencing filing, a clear mark should be made with a scriber and referred to at regular intervals. When a lot of metal has to be removed, do not be tempted to file out a section and then move to the next piece. Remove a little metal from the whole of the length and keep repeating until the final line is reached. If the finished job is to be a straight line, constantly check with a straight edge, such as a steel ruler, that light does not show between the straight edge and the work.

When filing to a radius, as well as carefully marking a line to work to, it is a good idea to make a simple gauge from cardboard, and check against that before finally working to the line itself. When making a radius it is all too easy to take too much from one side and it is then difficult to get back to the required curve. The use of a template helps to keep the curve regular throughout its length. For internal curvature it will of course be necessary to use a half round or round file, while an ordinary

The file should be maintained at 90 degrees to the work and supported at the end to keep it on the correct plane. It must be lifted at the end of each stroke.

hand file can be used for external work. On smaller work, where a radius is required small lengths of silver steel of the correct radius can be parted off and hardened. They can then be stuck to the component and will act as a guide for the file, without the need to refer to a scribed line. Whether the radius is internal or external, it is more often than not an advantage to make the finishing cuts with a draw filing action.

Draw Filing

Draw filing is the technique used to get a good clean and accurate finish to an edge. It in some ways contravenes what has already been written about the cutting action of the teeth of the file, as it is moved sideways along work, and so the normal cutting edge is not brought into use at all. Although the back of the teeth do not come into contact with the metal either, pressure should still be relieved on the back stroke, otherwise it is difficult to judge the exact amount of metal that is being removed.

File Construction

Like most things, if we have some knowledge of how a file is constructed it helps towards a better understanding of why it should be used in a certain way. Files are made of hardened metal with teeth that are relieved at the back, in

much the same way as are the teeth of a saw blade. In fact, a file is like a series of saw blades, joined closely to each other sideways, although the stagger is slightly oblique rather than square, and in most instances a second row of teeth crosses over at an angle of 60 degrees. Files are available in a variety of shapes to suit individual purposes and generally in three degrees of coarseness, known as smooth, second cut and bastard. There are additions to this range with some files available to give a particularly heavy cut (described as having milled teeth), and a range of very fine files graded from zero to four. Various lengths are obtainable, very small ones being called needle files. Slightly larger but still small files are called warding files. Some small files, about the size of needle files, have curved ends and are known as rifflers, and are very useful in places where a tiny radius is needed. Most files used for general purposes have a pointed tang on the end that is designed to fit into a handle, which have customarily been made of wood. The tang of the file is heated and driven into the handle, the heating process being sufficient to burn a passage into the handle. Attempting to drive the file in cold will more often than not cause the handle to split. More recently, plastic handles have become available and these are designed so that the file can be pushed straight in, giving the advantage that they are easily removed and can be fitted to another file. It is possible to purchase a type of file with a rounded end that acts as a handle, and these are often sold as blacksmith's files. They also have a

hole in the handle end that allows them to be hung up, which is very useful for storage purposes. Under no circumstances whatever should a file with a tang on it be used without fitting a handle first – to do so is a very dangerous practice indeed and can cause nasty injuries. The same warning applies to files that have handles that are split. A split is only one degree away from no handle at all and is even more dangerous as a false sense of safety is present because there is a handle, albeit a very dangerous one.

It is possible to buy files in sets when several different shapes are supplied, sometimes in a plastic wallet; it is far better though to buy what one wants as it is needed. For example, if one bought a set of 8in files (files still do not seem to have been metricated), it is highly probably that one of the shapes would be needed in a smaller version and the one in the set never used. When buying good quality files – and good quality must be stressed, as inferior ones become useless in no time at all – there is little, if any, saving in cost by buying a set. It is likely that some of the files will never be used, and in any case it is rare to see really good quality files sold in this fashion. Always get them from a reputable tool dealer where quality can be assured and more often than not expert advice is available.

Although all too frequently not treated as such, files are precision tools and great care should be taken to keep them in good condition. They should not just be thrown in a drawer, as the action of one file against the

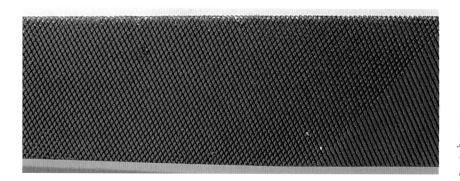

The pattern of teeth usually found on a file – the rows cross each other at an angle of 60 degrees.

Above *A needle file used to clean a casting; note that the file does not have a tang and can therefore be safely used without a handle.*

Below *Using a riffler (curved file) to clean an awkward, confined space.*

other will soon remove the cutting edge. If they are to be kept in a drawer, partitions should be made so that they will each have their own place. These need not go the full length of the drawer; even a series of pieces of dowel will do so long as it prevents the files getting damaged.

When we come to dealing with drills you will read that tools used on brass should not be kept in an ultra sharp condition, as this will cause a snatching effect that will ruin work. When it comes to both filing and sawing, exactly the opposite applies and for cutting brass the tools should be as sharp as possible. If a saw blade or file has been used on steel it should never be used on brass, as doing so results in a tendency for the teeth to skate across the work. When it comes to filing this results not only in difficulty in filing, but also when a large surface area is worked on, considerable scoring occurs that becomes very difficult or even impossible to remove. A good idea is to keep brand new files and saw blades for working on brass and when it becomes necessary to use them on steel, just mark them and do not ever try to use them on brass again. An ideal material for marking is typing correction fluid, as the white shows up easily and it is quick drying. Paint, of course, can be used, but there is always the difficulty of keeping the brush clean and the much longer drying time must be considered.

Cleaning Files

Over a period of time, file teeth become clogged and need to be cleaned. This applies particularly to steel and aluminium, but less so to brass, and in the case of the latter material a good sharp tap of the file edge on a wooden block will frequently be all that is needed to remove any residue. Aluminium and its associated alloys are invariably difficult material to work with, and because of their low melting point tend to stick to any cutting tool during use. Steel poses an entirely different problem, as slivers get caught in the teeth and the friction motion when filing causes them to work-harden. The file will then score any metal it is

used on, and so frequent removal of the slivers is essential. We do see advertised short wire brushes for file cleaning purposes, but in spite of the results claimed by the manufacturers or retailers they should be avoided at all costs. Some have hardened steel bristles, but even if the bristles are soft they will work-harden in no time at all and ultimately damage the teeth. The way to get rid of both steel and aluminium impregnated in the teeth is to take a small scrap of brass sheet, about 1.5mm thick, and ease the slivers out individually, using a diagonal motion. It does not take long and it will keep the file in good condition. When a file becomes too worn for these methods to work, it is sometimes possible to restore it by leaving it soaking in a mild solution of hydrochloric acid for a couple of days, which has the effect of dissolving the minute particles of dirt that have caused the clogging.

Prevention is Better Than Cure

The above cleaning methods work quite well, but it is far better to prolong the life of files rather than restoring them, and although nothing will ultimately prevent wear, there are some tricks that will help to keep them in reasonable condition. The first is to cover the surface with ordinary blackboard chalk by rubbing it briskly over the whole surface, which prevents dust and slivers from sticking in between the teeth. A similar effect can be obtained by using washing-up liquid. Application of a cutting oil during operations can also prevent heartaches later, but use one of the thicker oils, rather than the soluble type which do not seem to be stable enough for the job. Do not use oil when filing brass or copper.

Non-Standard Files

Most files are still made in basically the same way as they were a couple of hundred years ago, which just goes to prove their effectiveness, but while much in engineering is traditional those engaged in it are constantly seeking new ways to go about things. In recent years this has

Extra Precision

Keeping a file perfectly flat is very difficult indeed, and one way to achieve this without too much trouble is to make a small roller to fit on the vice. It just requires two brackets that are bolted to the sides of the vice, for which a couple of small holes may have to be drilled and tapped. The roller is best made from nylon or a similar plastic, as steel and brass tend to wear quickly.

Right *A roller fitted to a vice – using it ensures that the file remains level across the work.*

Below *The roller as seen when taken off the vice. Slots in the arms fit screws that are in tapped holes made in the vice casting.*

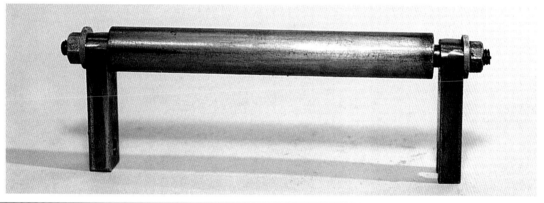

resulted in a completely new type of file coming on the market, which instead of the traditional teeth has a large number of tiny pieces of tungsten or diamond set in it. There are no teeth such as such, which means the file will cut in both directions. This appears to make a nonsense of all that has so far been written, but such files are limited in their uses. While they will remove metal quite well and so are quite good for rough work, it is difficult to get a good smooth finish with them. No doubt in the future the idea will supersede the more traditional type of file, but this could be quite a long way off.

Differing from the normal type of file, this is a diamond-coated one. Small segments of industrial diamonds have been stuck to the base and act as the cutting medium instead of the usual teeth. Because of the random pattern of the diamonds, it is safe to cut both backwards and forwards with this type of file.

It can be difficult to get the necessary degree of precision when working on very tiny components, as there is always a tendency for a rocking motion as the file passes over the work. It is sometimes possible to use the drilling machine to correct this. Start by disconnecting it from the main supply and releasing the drive belts so that the mandrel runs free, put a needle file in the chuck and set the work on a suitable block, moving the file up and down by means of the machine while passing the work along, using a suitable guide. The files stays perfectly perpendicular, ensuring an exact 90-degree edge, and by setting the mounting block at an angle it is also possible to make a consistent angle, something that is very difficult to do using normal filing methods. It is an idea that works particularly well when a small slot or a square hole is needed, as both are difficult to make by more normal methods.

Scrapers

One other method of removing metal that should be mentioned is scraping. Like so many other things, it is rapidly becoming a lost art. Once it was the only way used to ensure a perfectly flat surface, but now the use of machines like surface grinders has left little need for it. In fact, although it will from time to time be a means to an end, it is unlikely that there is going to be any need for the scraping of large areas. Scrapers take several forms, the most common one being very much like a wood chisel. Because of its shape, it is quite common for it to be made by grinding off the end of a worn-out file. The action of using the scraper is to push it along the work, and if tiny high spots need to be removed it is generally far more accurate than filing.

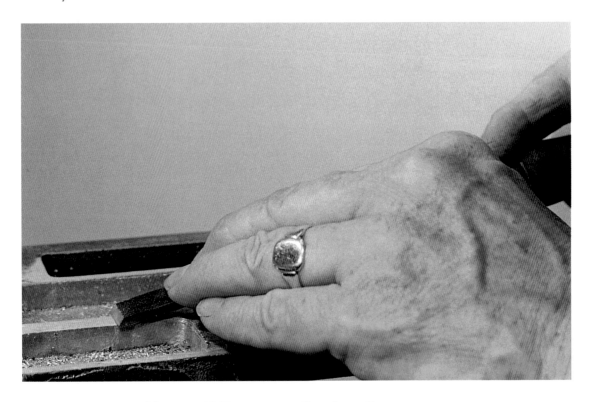

Using a scraper, ground from an old file, to ensure a flat-edge surface on an aluminium casting.

FINISHING WITH ABRASIVES

Although an extremely good finish can be obtained on any metal by the correct use of a file, particularly one of the very smooth range, many people prefer to do their final finishing with abrasives, such as emery paper and the like. We are now blessed with several types of abrasive that can be used in a machine and can save a lot of work. Information about these is set out below.

Abrasive Papers and Cloths

Abrasives are generally used in the workshop in the form of paper and cloth, on which there is a coating of tiny particles of material that are very sharp. Once it was only emery cloth or paper that was used, but now there is now a much wider range of coatings. Particularly popular are the sheets made with a surface of aluminium oxide, which can generally be recognized by their brown finish. They have the advantage of being longer lasting than emery. Also worth considering are the silicon carbide papers frequently known as 'wet and dry', which were originally made for the motorcar industry. These too have good cutting ability, and if used in conjunction with a little water or oil will give a very fine finish on steel and brass. All abrasive sheets are available in a wide range of varying coarseness – there are eleven different grades of aluminium oxide material alone, so it can be seen that the range is vast.

How abrasive papers or cloth are used will depend on the particular situation. For cleaning small objects it is a good idea to fold the cloth or paper round a file so that there is a flat surface to work with. Clock-makers use buffing sticks that consist of very fine abrasive paper stuck to a piece of flat wood, and there is no reason why this idea cannot be copied in metalworking. In the case of internal radii, a round or half round file can be used to support the material with equal effect, or it could be stuck to a piece of dowel. If a large flat surface is to be cleaned, particularly if it is necessary to get it absolutely flat, lay the material on a known flat and true surface, abrasive side up, and work the metal over it in a figure of eight motion. Do not try to push it backwards and forwards, as there is every possibility that a slight rocking motion will be set up and the finished surface will not be perfectly flat.

ABRASIVE BLOCKS

It is possible to obtain abrasive material bonded into blocks. The bonding material is much softer than that of a grindstone and the blocks easily start to wear, which is exactly what they are designed to do. The idea is that they will take up the shape of the object being cleaned and thereby get into recesses. They are ideal for the purpose, and can even be cut into small pieces in order to clean and polish areas that are otherwise inaccessible.

FIBRE HAND PADS

Ideal for final cleaning and polishing, as well as for rust removal, are fibre hand pads, generally sold under the name of Scotchbrite. Like so many other abrasive materials they are identified by their colour, which not only indicates the material the pad is made from, but also how coarse it is. The colours are as follows. White – very fine and mainly used for polishing metal that has previously been dealt with, using another grade. Grey – extra fine, for light finishing on all metals and ideal as a key for paint or lacquer; the pads are made with silicon carbide. Green – also extra fine but a little coarser than grey; made of aluminium silicate and particularly useful for removing rust and other forms of corrosion. Maroon – fine, particularly good for putting a fine finish on non-ferrous metals and stainless steels; the abrasive material is aluminium oxide. Black – medium grade, good for removal of scratches from steels; the abrasive material is silicon carbide. Brown – coarse grade, made with aluminium oxide and ideal for finishing steels where machining marks remain; the grade can also be used for deburring the edges of sheet metal.

A flap wheel. Consisting of a series of folded pieces of abrasive cloth, the wheel is very useful for cleaning and preparing contoured surfaces.

MECHANICAL ABRASIVES

There are other mechanically driven abrasives that might be of use in certain forms of work. Most are used with a portable electric drill or a flexible drive. For example, it is possible to obtain mounted points that are small stones made in various shapes and fixed to an arbor. They are specially designed for use with flexible drives. The stones are very useful for cleaning castings or the joins on work that has been assembled by welding or brazing. Flap wheels consist of layers of abrasive paper folded concertina fashion and shaped into a wheel secured to an arbor. They are available in various grades, and are also used in a portable drill or with a flexible drive to provide a quick way of cleaning contoured work. Sanding drums consist of soft, drum-shaped, flexible pads wrapped round an arbor. A circular band of abrasive material fits on the pad, which results is an extremely flexible device that is also capable of taking up the contour of the work; the drums are available in a variety of diameters. In addition, most readers will know of the widely used sanding disc, which is fitted to a backplate and used in a portable drill. These are useful for heavy work but somewhat limited when it comes to attempting to get a fine finish, as they tend to leave unwanted circular marks in the metal. All the above devices are available in a variety of grades of material.

A popular finish is one described as engine turning. A piece of wooden dowel is fitted into the chuck of a drilling machine and the work is given a very light coating of a mild abrasive such as a brass polish. The machine is started and the dowel brought into contact with the work in a series of short sharp jabs. It is moved about half the width of the dowel after each jab. The result is a quite pleasing effect of circular marks alternating between a flat and polished finish.

This lathe filing rest has been finished by the process of engine turning, which results in an attractive pattern of small whorls all over the surface.

5 Threading

Making threads is a very important part of metalworking. There are few, if any, aspects of the subject that will not from time to time require a thread of some sort to be made. Threading will also be dealt with in Chapter Eight, but in that case it is in relation to operations with the lathe – making threads at the bench requires entirely different techniques altogether and that is what we will deal with in this chapter.

STANDARDS

Whether threads are going to be made by machine or by hand at the bench, it is useful to have an understanding of the various types, which fortunately, as a result of some degree of standardization, is a subject nowhere as complex as it used to be. For many years, the craftsman made threads to whatever size and form he wished, and if whatever he had made went to someone else for repair it would be most unfortunate because the repairer would have no idea as to what the threads were. In 1842, Sir Joseph Whitworth introduced a standard to the engineering industry that was to be universally adopted in Great Britain and most of the world, and was to remain in use for many years to come. Restorers of old machinery and motor vehicles will be only too aware of the Whitworth Thread, known by the initials BSW, as it was used extensively throughout the engineering industry.

A thread is measured in two ways, by the outside diameter of the bolt and by the number of threads along a given distance, now more generally known as the pitch. The Whitworth system was very coarse and further development produced a much finer version known as British Standard Fine or BSF. For even smaller and finer work, an approach was made to the watchmaking trade in Switzerland to design yet another set of standards. It is not clear why Switzerland was chosen as the place where the standard was to be designed, when watchmakers in Britain were already beginning to standardize their own threads, but the end result was a very useful standard, known as the British Association Thread or BA. Although the use of BA threads was to become popular throughout the world for many years, it has always been a rather odd system, the measurements being something of a cross between metric and imperial. All three standards have now officially been superseded and metric forms adopted, but it is essential to know about them as many drawings still specify their use and restorers of old equipment will find that they have been extensively used. Fortunately, there is no difficulty in buying taps and dies for these threads, so they are definitely still with us, even if their role has been reduced.

The metric thread form was designed in 1898 and gradually became the accepted standard throughout Europe. These days we find metric threads are specified for products made in Britain and most other parts of the world. The major exception to this is the United States, where after a period of using the three British Standards two new ones were devised. These are known as American National Coarse (ANC) and American National Fine (ANF), and are rather confusingly also referred to as Unified Coarse (UNC) and Unified Fine (UNF). Nearly all machinery, including motor vehicles, made during the twentieth century in America and a great deal of the Far East as well, has these threads. As if all these thread forms were not bad enough, another rather confusing standard was set up for use in industries where pipework was involved. Called British Standard Pipe (BSP), its use was not by any means confined to Britain and it is still used today all over the world. There are yet more standards, although one is less likely to meet with them. The whole system is very complicated, but will mainly concern restorers, as those making items from scratch will be able to decide what thread to use for themselves, and those shown on old drawings can always be replaced with something similar.

THREAD FORMS

As well as the outside diameter and pitch there is another factor to be considered when dealing with threads – their form, or the angles of the spirals that do the work. For threads that are used on nuts and bolts as a means of joining parts together, the thread form is triangular. Although the angles of the sides of the triangle might vary, it is quite common to use threads as a source of power rather than for holding parts together. The basic triangular form is not suited to this type of work and it is more usual to use either a square or acme form. The latter has a steep angle and a square top, allowing greater pressure to be applied than is possible with a triangular form.

Threads for Measuring

Threads are also extensively used as a means of measuring. We see numerous examples of this

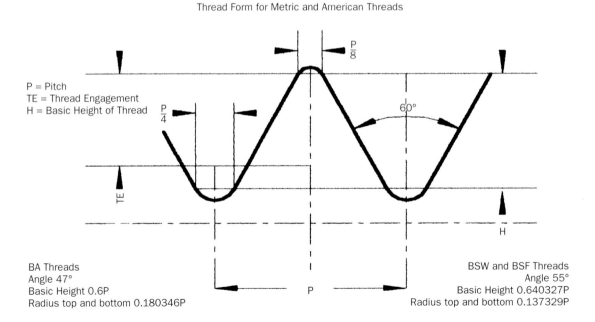

Thread Form for Metric and American Threads

P = Pitch
TE = Thread Engagement
H = Basic Height of Thread

$\frac{P}{8}$

$\frac{P}{4}$

60°

TE

H

BA Threads
Angle 47°
Basic Height 0.6P
Radius top and bottom 0.180346P

P

BSW and BSF Threads
Angle 55°
Basic Height 0.640327P
Radius top and bottom 0.137329P

Chart showing the angles and radii of regularly used threads. The metric and American forms are identical, although diameters and pitches differ.

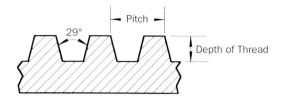

Square Thread
This type of thread is only used as a drive mechanism. It is impossible to make with taps and dies and very difficult to screw cut on a lathe

Acme Thread
Generally used for light drives. The acme type of thread is likely to be found on lathes

The square thread is used for drive mechanisms. The depth is equal to half the pitch.

Commonly used for lead screws on machines, the acme thread is a compromise between the standard and square forms. It cannot be made without the use of a machine, but it is possible to obtain special taps for general maintenance purposes.

in the workshop – micrometers that measure with extreme accuracy do so entirely from the rotation of the thread, and there are lead screws on machines that actually do a double job because they provide power as well as measurement. What all this means is that if we have a thread with a pitch of 1mm, that is, each complete turn of the thread is 1mm in length, it follows that by turning the screw a certain number of times we have a very precise measurement of the distance something connected to it will have travelled. Lead screw graduations and micrometers work on the principle of fitting a collar with a number of divisions to the thread; the movement through these divisions equals a partial turn of the thread and so a partial distance travelled. For example, if the thread has a pitch of 1mm we know that is the distance it will travel on a full turn. If the collar has ten divisions, the movement through each of these divisions is equal to one-tenth of a revolution of the screw and therefore 0.1mm.

Strength of Threads

In theory, a coarse-threaded bolt or screw is weaker than one with a fine thread. This is because the coarse thread is deeper than a fine

one and so the basic diameter of the bolt is weakened. For example, if we take the root diameter of a 20mm bolt it is nearly 17mm; in the case of the same diameter for fine thread it is more like 19mm. Therefore if the bolt is put in a position where the stresses on it are across the diameter, then the finer thread is stronger. Look at it from another angle and the reverse situation arises – if the stresses are against the length of the bolt, the coarse thread is the stronger.

TAPPING DRILLS

The pitch and type of thread also has a bearing on its depth and we need to know a little about this. In the case of an internal thread there is no point in drilling a hole of the diameter of the bolt that is to be fitted, because it cannot be converted into a thread. It is necessary to drill an undersized hole of the diameter equal to the bottom of the grooves; it cannot just be any undersized hole, but has to be reasonably precise, equal to the outside diameter of the thread minus its pitch. For example, if the thread is 6mm diameter and has a pitch of 1mm the drill needed for tapping will be 5mm. When working with metric threads it is a very simple calculation, but if we are to use any of the imperial standards it is a different matter altogether, as these are known by the number of threads per inch. In order to obtain the pitch first it is necessary to divide the number of threads into an inch and then to take the result away from the diameter in order to get the size of the correct tapping drill. That is complicated enough, but few of the pitches will work out to an exact fraction of an inch and so it will be necessary to use a metric drill and it now becomes a case of working out which is the nearest to the figure given in imperial terms. It all sounds and indeed is quite complicated and the best idea is to use a suitable chart where somebody else has already done all the calculations for you. A number of these charts will be found in the appendix, and it is a good idea to copy them on to a piece of card, cover it in plastic and put it on a wall in the workshop for easy reference. It is only necessary to use the particular tables that relate to the threads in normal use and these will vary with individual needs.

In some cases it may be necessary to use a slightly different size to that shown, depending on the quality of thread required. A thread is said to have an engagement of so many per cent depending on how close fitting it needs to be. A screw that is wanted for quick release, such as on a clamp, would have an engagement of about 80 per cent or even slightly less, while with one that has to be water-tight the engagement should be nearer to 100 per cent. In general, the charts show about 90 per cent, which means that it is quite permissible to use a

size larger drill if only 80 per cent is required, and one size smaller if a tighter fit is needed. The size of tapping drill should also vary with the material being tapped. The figures given generally work well on steel, but a size smaller should be used on brass and a size larger on material such as copper and aluminium that tend to spread rather than cut.

CLEARANCE-SIZED DRILLS

Usually the size of drill to be used for clearance is the same or slightly larger than the outside diameter of the thread. If a thread is 10mm in diameter and a 10mm drill is used for clearance, the bolt should go through and give a nice snug fit. Sometimes it is not a snug fit that is needed – it might be necessary to have a larger amount of clearance, particularly where a number of bolt holes are concerned, and in this case an increase in the clearance-sized drill is quite permissible. At the same time, clearance holes should not be enlarged in order to make up for lack of accuracy.

LINING UP THE HOLES

If a component is being made that will bolt to another it can call for a whole series of holes to be made that match each other. They need to be tapping size on one piece and clearance on the other. There is really no substitute for measuring very accurately and getting them all correct, but this is not easy to achieve. In these circumstances, drill all the tapping-sized holes and thoroughly deburr them, clamp the two plates together and use the pre-drilled one as a jig to drill the other. Next, separate them and open out the holes in the second plate to clearance size – they should all match up perfectly.

TAPS

Although taps are available in three forms – taper, second and plug or bottoming, the latter name depending on the area in which one

---

Non-Standard Threads

No doubt there will be some people who will be doing work of one type or another that will include the use of threads that have not been covered. Unfortunately, there are so many variations that it is not practical to cover them all and if that is the case it will be necessary to calculate the size of drill required for oneself.

lives – it is generally quite possible to make acceptable threads using only two and dispensing with the second cut type. The thread is first of all made with a taper tap and the plug used to bring it to full diameter along the whole of its length. Taps are obtainable made from carbon or high-speed steel and for most work the latter has to be recommended as these have a much longer life than the carbon ones. However, occasionally one might wish to tap a hole to a size which is very unlikely to ever be used again, and it is hard to justify the expense of buying a high-speed steel one in that case and for just a few holes the carbon steel tap is quite suitable. In Chapter Ten, a method of sharpening taps is described.

Tapping

The tap should be held in a good tap wrench and after one or two revolutions, reversed and brought away from the work to clear the swarf, before proceeding with the next turn or two, then repeating the operation. The appropriate cutting fluid should always be used, that means a tapping compound for steel and paraffin for brass or aluminium. Copper is very difficult to

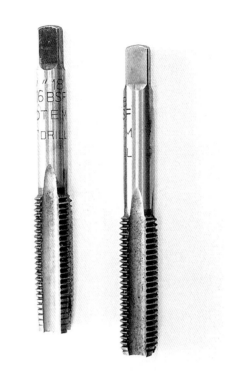

A pair of taps (taper and plug); the taper, shown on the left, is used to start a thread.

A small tap with a home-made tap wrench. At the bottom is a brass sleeve that is used as a guide to prevent the tap slipping to an angle. The guide is held to the work as hard as possible and the tap passes through it. The flat end keeps the guide and therefore the tap at 90 degrees to the work.

tap as the swarf gets trapped in the flutes and unfortunately it will remain there when the rotation is reversed; rather surprisingly one of the best liquids to use as a cutting compound on copper to prevent sticking is milk.

Tapping Blind Holes

So far, it has been assumed that the hole being tapped is going right through the metal, allowing the tap to protrude from the opposite side. In the case of a tapping a blind hole, there is the danger of it binding in the hole and breaking. To do one's best to prevent this sort of accident, the bottom of the hole should be cut square with a 'D' bit and thoroughly cleaned out before tapping commences; also the tapping drill should be a size larger than would have been used if the hole were clear. Carefully measure the depth of the hole and note the number of complete revolutions it will take for the tap to reach the end. For example, if the hole is 10mm deep and the thread has a pitch of 1mm, it will take exactly ten revolutions to reach the bottom. Just to make sure, wrap a piece of insulation tape round the threads of the taps at the position equal to ten revolutions; there is now a visible guide in addition to counting the number of revolutions used. Tapping can be carried out in exactly the same way as one would for a through hole, except that it will be necessary to keep clearing the swarf from the bottom of the hole.

Keeping Taps Upright

To anyone not used to tapping it would seem that holding the tap at 90 degrees to the work is very simple, but that is not the case and one of the major causes of tap breakage is because a tap enters the hole at an angle. It is quite difficult to see when it is happening as taps are invariably dwarfed by the wrench that is used to work them and are mainly hidden from view during operations. While care may have been taken that the tap was started at a true 90 degrees, it is likely to move to an angle during operations. Not only is this a source of broken taps, but it also means that the bolt or stud that

---

Getting a Good Start

One reason for taps going into the work at an angle is a burr that is left when the hole is drilled, as the raised metal can push the tap out of line. Not only must the work be completely deburred, but it is also a good idea to make a tiny countersink in which the tap may be given a start.

---

is to fit in the hole protrudes at an angle, which can result in it not lining up accurately with the mating part, as well as looking very untidy.

STAKING TOOLS

The tool used to ensure that taps are maintained at the correct angle is called a staking tool and invariably these are made in the workshop to suit one's own individual requirements. They are really very simple, consisting of a base with a column at a true 90 degrees. On the column is a crosspiece, which is adjustable for height and has a second hole for a bearing. Through the bearing is a shaft or mandrel that has a fitting at one end that is capable of accepting the tap. It is fitted at the top with a tommy bar. The work is laid on the base and the tap operated by the tommy bar in the same way as when an ordinary wrench is used.

GUIDES

It is not always possible to use a drilling machine or staking tool, usually because the workpiece is too large to fit underneath. In such cases, a simple guide can be used to assist in keeping a tap at 90 degrees. This consists of nothing more than a piece of bar material, faced to a true 90 degrees and drilled with a hole that is a close clearance for the tap shank. The larger the area round the hole, the better the guide will work as it is easier to maintain the correct angle. The guides can be stored in a box and used time and time again.

Using the Drilling Machine

The amount of equipment gathered in a workshop over a period of years increases at an alarming rate and so there might not be room to house a staking tool. A similar effect can be obtained by using the drilling machine. A length of tube is placed in the chuck and the tap mounted in a small holder that is a good running fit in the tube. It is an easy set-up to make and can be used in the tailstock of the lathe as well as in the drilling machine.

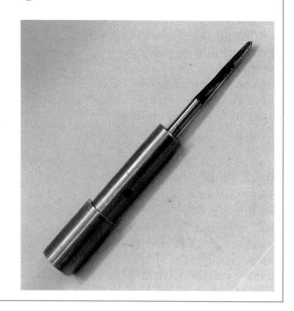

The tap in this photograph has been secured in a length of steel with a retaining compound and that in turn fits into a brass sleeve. The sleeve is mounted in the chuck of a bench drill and the tap rotated by hand. Because it can slide up and down in the sleeve as well as rotate, there is no need to move the spindle of the machine, which must be switched off.

DIES

Types of Die

Except when made with the use of a lathe, external threads are made by using a die, which is held in a die holder, or stock as it is sometimes called. In Great Britain it is usual to use split dies. The holder for these has three screws set at an angle of 45 degrees to each other and in theory at least this allows some adjustment to the outside diameter of the thread. A great deal of pressure is required to thread metal using a die, and by using a split one it is possible to remove a lesser amount on the first cut and then adjust the die to the correct size when making a second or even third cut. Very few countries other than Britain use this type of die; the reason is almost certainly because it is sometimes possible to over-tighten when adjusting for the final cut and finish up with an undersized thread. There is nothing at all wrong with them, they will cut a perfectly

A small tap guide. Made from mild steel, it has a nice wide base to ensure it stays at 90 degrees. It is also knurled to enable it to be held without rotating.

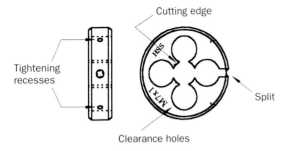

A drawing of a standard split die as used in Great Britain. Dies are available in diameters of $\frac{13}{16}$in; 1in; $1\frac{5}{16}$in; $1\frac{1}{2}$in and 2in. Strangely, these sizes are standard no matter whether the thread the die will cut is metric or imperial.

good thread when used by hand, although their primary use is in machines. Die Nuts are as the name suggests, dies with a hexagonal periphery. They are not split and their main use is in the restoration of damaged threads, when they can be operated with a spanner rather than a stock.

Using the Die

In many ways, using a die is similar to using a tap. It needs to be rotated for a revolution or two and then released, by reversing the movement. Where appropriate, a lubricant should always be used. Swarf is just as much a problem with a die as it is with a tap, and care must be taken to keep clearing it. Although a die does not break as easily as a tap, it is still quite possible that it will if it becomes jammed and force is applied. If possible, a small lead should be filed on the work before starting to use the die in order to give it a start, but care must be taken to ensure that the lead is even all

the way round the metal, otherwise the die will start at an angle. The two sides of a die differ; one has a small lead, whereas the other is nearly flat. Always commence by using the side with the lead, which is the one that will have the name of the manufacturer and size stamped on it, as this allows for easier starting of the thread. While from this point of view the lead is an advantage, it prevents the die from making a thread right up to a shoulder and will always leave a very short length unthreaded. Having completed operations the die can be reversed in the holder and the blank side used to extend the thread to the shoulder.

As with a tap, there is a very real problem when threading with a die that it will run at an angle. Fortunately, it is easier to see what one is doing as a rule and so to be able to correct this. A small square can often be held against the work to ensure that the die is at exactly 90 degrees and that the angle is maintained throughout the length of the thread.

One cause of a die cutting at an angle is failure to set it accurately in the stock; a small piece of swarf or even careless positioning can create enough of an angle on the die to make it difficult to work with.

Using a Lining-Up Piece

Although a small square has been suggested as a means of lining the die accurately, frequently these can prove to be too large for the job. It might be found more convenient to cut a piece of flat mild steel of a suitable size and ensure that the edges are at exactly 90 degrees and use that instead.

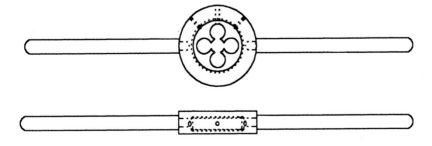

Drawing of a typical die holder or stock, showing position of the three securing screws for the die. Making such a stock is a simple project.

6 Drills and Drilling

The word drill is used to describe both the twist drill that makes the hole and the machine that causes it to rotate; mainly this chapter will concern itself with the twist drill rather than the machine. Basically, a drill is a twisted piece of metal, with a point on the end. For many years, the tiny drills used by clock and watchmakers were referred to as wire drills and were literally a piece of twisted wire. This is of course no longer the case, as much higher quality steels are used and drills are made by a different process to much higher tolerances than they used to be.

SIZES

The range of drills available is incredible – apart from diameters that go from as thin as a human hair to the size of a plate, they vary in length and design, certain types giving the best results in different circumstances. Once again, it must be repeated that the best results come from good quality, as the cheap ones sold on market stalls tend to be far too brittle and will break easily and those sold in DIY stores are generally not of a true size. To clarify the latter point, if one goes into a DIY store for a drill, say for the sake of argument $\frac{1}{8}$in diameter, the packet in which it is sold will state $\frac{1}{8}$in or 3mm diameter. These measurements are not the same by any means and while the drill might well do for DIY work, where the hole is probably just to hammer a dowel into, a far greater precision is needed when it comes to metalwork.

If a project is being made from an old drawing, readers might be confused to find that hole sizes are quoted in numbers or letters. These relate to a series of drills once used in Great Britain and North America, where numbers went from one to eighty, with one the largest at about $\frac{1}{4}$in in diameter and eighty slightly smaller than $\frac{1}{64}$in. There was no logical progression in the series, but it had the advantage of offering a wide diversity of sizes. Letter-sized drills went from A–Z, starting with A as the smallest. Although specialist suppliers still market the ranges, it is more convenient to use the nearest metric equivalent.

The drawing shows how a drill is made. The cutting edge has an included angle of 118 degrees and there is also a clearance angle, which provides clearance for the chip or swarf, as well as strengthening the cutting edge. The spiral flutes are also obviously to help clear away swarf. It will be noted that there is a slight lip, known as the land or margin, along the outer edge of the spiral. A common error is to believe that this is also a cutting edge and attempting to use it as a sort of milling cutter; it is only for clearance and has no cutting properties whatever.

SPECIAL SPIRALS

The angle of the flutes is known as the helix angle and can vary according to the work for which the drill is designed. Slow helix drills have a shallow angle and are specially designed for drilling brass and similar non-ferrous metals, or some types of plastic. If designed for

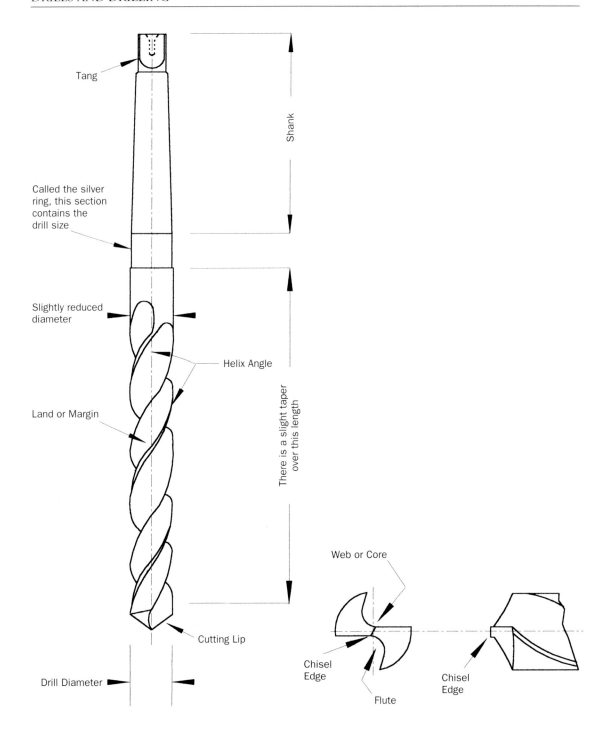

Tang

Called the silver
ring, this section
contains the
drill size

Slightly reduced
diameter

Land or Margin

Shank

Helix Angle

There is a slight taper
over this length

Web or Core

Cutting Lip

Drill Diameter

Chisel
Edge

Flute

Chisel
Edge

*A drawing showing the make-up of a twist drill
and the angles required for the majority of work.*

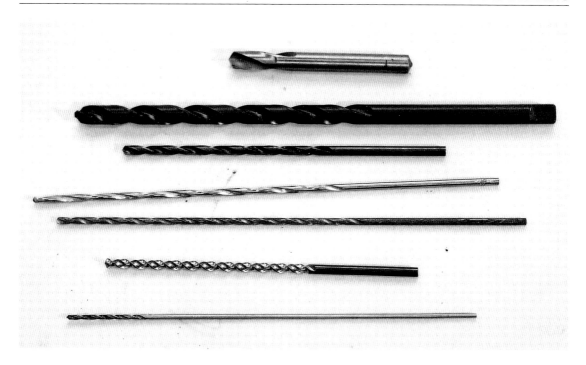

plastic, the cutting angle will be 60 degrees. Generally in the home workshop the standard drill is used for all purposes, it not being practical to purchase special types for every job.

LONG DRILLS

Long series and extra long series drills speak for themselves. They are of additional length for extra deep holes, but can be useful for drilling holes in spaces where there is limited access. In the case of extra deep holes, the long series drill should follow one of a standard length and in the case of the extra long series, used both standard and long series before the extra long one. Very short drills are known as stub drills and are less likely to flex than ordinary drills, making them useful on hard materials. It is not advisable to be tempted to make a stub drill by cutting a standard one down to size. The web of a drill increases in thickness as it recedes from the point, in order to give added strength ,and if a drill is reduced to half its normal length the web thickness is increased and must be reduced when the drill is sharpened. This usually

The photograph shows a variety of special-purpose drills. From top to bottom: a stub drill; two standard long series drills; an extra long series slow helix; standard extra long series; a long series quick helix; and an extended drill with a long plain shank.

involves the use of a very slim grindstone and the grinding must be done very accurately to ensure that the web is evenly spaced either side of the point.

DRILL MATERIALS

Although most drills are made from high-speed steel, it is possible to obtain some made from more modern materials, which for some work can have considerable advantages. No doubt we are all familiar with masonry drills that have a tungsten carbide section brazed on the tip in order that they will drill into concrete and similar hard materials. These are not suitable for metalworking because of the way they are manufactured, but it is possible to obtain a full range of solid tungsten carbide drills that will

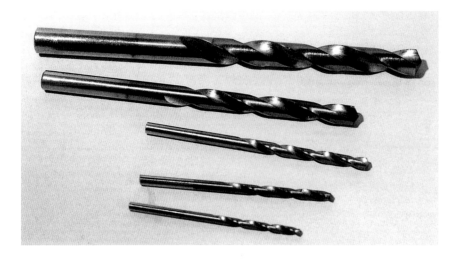

These TiN-coated drills have a distinctive colour. They give a quicker release of swarf and remain sharper for longer periods that ordinary high-speed drills.

cut into harder materials that would instantly blunt the ordinary high-speed drill. These drills need to be run at considerably higher speeds than usual and because of this it is usually only possible to use very small ones. They must be treated very carefully, particularly where small diameters are concerned as they snap very easily. Drills manufactured from cobalt can also be useful where hard material is to be drilled. Possibly of more use to the person working in a small workshop will be high-speed drills with a coating of titanium, designated as titanium nitride drills and always referred to as TiN. The coating enables quicker release of material, thus improving cutting qualities and therefore generating less heat. Tools made this way have a distinctive gold colour.

DRILLING MACHINES

In the introduction to this book it was shown how within living memory the person doing metalwork for a hobby frequently had few machines with which to work —nowadays there can be very few who do not have a drilling machine of some sort or another. Even if a specially designed machine is not available, those without will almost certainly have a hand-held power drill for which a stand can either be bought or made. The main advantage of any machine, even the hand-held one on a stand, is that it will be possible to set a drill at 90 degrees to the work and be sure of a reasonable degree of accuracy.

Purpose-designed machines come in a very wide range of sizes; some are floor-standing models, while others stand on a bench, Unfortunately, the drill is a machine that can in the wrong hands suffer a lot of abuse, particularly in a factory, and so look carefully before buying second-hand. Check to see if there are any holes in the table, where it has not been properly lined up and the drill has gone into it. The table always has a central hole for the drill to pass through and frequently when it is not properly lined up a drill will strike the edge of that hole. If pressure is applied the drill bends or moves, making an angled groove. This enlarges the top of the hole, and in many cases it will be found that there are several of these places all round the central hole. Such damage need not be a bar to having the machine, however, as a thick steel plate can be put on top of the table to stabilize the workpiece. Check the bearings and see that there is little or if possible no sideways movement and check the rotation to see that the movement is concentric. Chucks are fitted via a Morse Taper and it should be possible to remove the chuck and feel inside the taper to ensure there is no scoring. If there is, at the best the machine will probably lack accuracy and at the worst the chuck will keep falling out during operations. If the table is of the type that does not adjust for tilt, put a drill or piece of round steel bar in the chuck and use a square to check that it is at 90 degrees to the table. How many, if any, faults the would-be purchaser is willing to tolerate is a personal matter, but it is worth remembering that it is now possible to purchase machines made in the Far East at remarkably low prices

and it might be better to do this than to buy a second-hand machine of dubious quality.

The diameter that the chuck will accept is always of interest; it is nice to have a chuck that will take large drills, but that same chuck will not be terribly good at holding small ones. Compromises can be made; a small drill can be held in a pin chuck, prior to fitting it into the chuck on the machine. Large drills are available

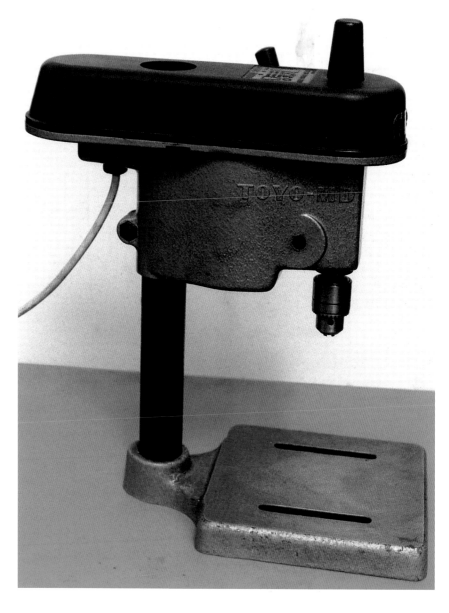

A small drilling machine with a maximum capacity of a 6mm drill. It is very useful for small workshops and delicate work.

A high quality drilling machine fitted with a cross slide in place of the more normal table. This allows work to be moved in both directions without having to remove it from the table.

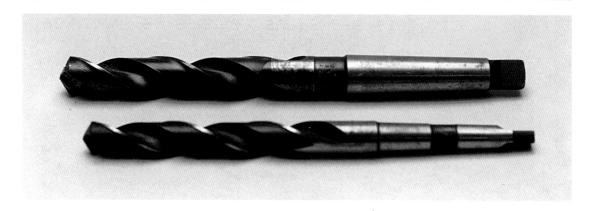

with Morse Tapers on the end to fit straight into the machine and can be used where the chuck is limited on size.

Drilling

Because of the chisel point on the drill it is difficult, if not impossible, to start drilling a hole accurately, and so a start should always be made using a centre drill of sufficient size to allow both ends of the chisel to enter the recess that has been made. It is frequent practice to make a centre-punch mark as a point to start

Large diameter drills with Morse Taper shanks, enabling them to be fitted directly into the mandrel of a drilling machine, the chuck of which would not accommodate them.

drilling, but it is very rare that the method will give an accurate result. When the metal is centre-punched, as well as an indent there is also raised edge round the mark. The periphery of this raised section will vary in height and will tend to push the drill to one side. A more rigid form of manufacture is employed when making

A selection of centre drills, the point of which should always be smaller than the diameter of the drill that is to be used.

97

centre drills, and as a result they are less prone to this movement and provide much greater accuracy.

During operations, the drill should be withdrawn at regular intervals to allow swarf to be cleared away, and if appropriate a cutting fluid should be employed. The drill must be rotating at as near the correct speed as is possible with the machine that is being used. A happy medium has to be struck between feeding it too quickly, which will cause it to dig into the metal and possibly break the drill, and not feeding fast enough, with the result that the drill rubs the metal instead of cutting into it and becomes overheated and blunt. Inevitably, there are limitations on the ability to use a machine running at the correct speed. Most drilling machines have about six different speeds, but cutting speeds are decided by the type of material being machined and the diameter of the drill. These limitations, plus the fact that it is more often than not impossible to discover what would be the correct speed for a particular type of metal, mean that we just have to compromise. The best advice that can be offered is: the smaller the diameter of the drill, the faster it should rotate; steel should be drilled at a slower speed than brass or aluminium; and copper must be drilled very slowly.

When drilling steel and aluminium it is essential to keep the drill as sharp as possible; however, when it comes to drilling copper and its various alloys, particularly brass, if a very sharp drill is used it is likely to snatch, particularly at the point where the drill starts to break through the metal. It is possible to grind drills especially to avoid this happening, but an easy solution is just to take the sharp edge off the drill, using a small oilstone. It is far easier to put an edge back on a drill after doing this than it is to return it to its original condition after regrinding.

Drilling Holes in Thin Sheet Metal

It is very difficult to drill a perfectly round hole in thin sheet metal – more often than not, the end result will take on an octagonal shape rather than circular and so a different technique to normal is required. Providing that the hole is not too large, up to say 12mm or 0.5in diameter, the problem can be cured by first spotting the hole position and putting a piece of cloth between the metal and the drill. The cloth rotates as it is contacted by the drill and prevents the drill snatching the metal and pulling it out of shape. An even better result can be obtained by using a piece of emery cloth between the drill and the work, but it must be emery cloth, not paper, as the latter only tears as the drill contacts it. Larger holes in thin sheet metal can be made using a type of drill normally sold for woodworking. Although it is not what this type of drill is designed for, the flat section cuts nicely through the metal, and being made of high-speed steel it will wear quite well. There are several commercial alternatives that are sold for such work. Some are like tapered files and others are made in a series of steps. Possibly the best of these commercial items is the hole saw, which consists of a saw blade shaped into a ring and fitted to a mandrel, through the centre of which is a pilot drill. The blades are available in various diameters, while the pilot drill is sized to work with any size of saw. If using a hole saw, do not forget that the initial pilot drill will have the same effect on thin sheet metal as any other drill, which means that steps must be taken to prevent it snatching as it breaks through. If this is not done, there is nothing to prevent the saw blade from wandering when it strikes the metal. It is also essential to use a very slow cutting speed and to feed the tool in very slowly.

For many years, the craftsman wanting large diameter holes in thin metal did not have the luxury of being able to buy such devices, and so chain drilling was resorted to. It was also the system used to cut sheet metal into shapes. It is a simple process and still remains one of the most accurate ways of getting truly accurate work. The hole required is scribed on the metal and another line is scribed inside it at a set distance; this is then carefully centre-punched

A series of holes drilled round in a circle. The size of the drills is gradually increased until the centre piece can be removed. The hole is then carefully finished to size with a file.

at regular intervals for drilling. The drill size should be such that the line of holes will break into each other and the outer diameter of the holes will be just short of the scribed line. When drilling is complete, the piece of metal will fall out and the remaining metal can be carefully removed with a file until the metal removed matches the required circle. To get the desired spacing the diameter of the scribed circle must be divided by the chord, which is the distance across the curved line from point to point; dividing the circumference does not work. Also if working on copper it is advisable to leave a tiny gap between the holes rather than try to break the holes into each other. The nature of the material is such that it work-hardens, which can throw the drill out of line, and the end result could possibly mean that the

drill will intersect the finishing line, rather than staying just short of it.

Holding the Work

All work must be securely held when carrying out drilling operations. If possible, hold it in a drilling vice, or if too large for that clamp the work securely to the drilling table. With odd-shaped components, however, neither of these alternatives is always practical, and a good option is to secure the work to a piece of wood and rest that on the drilling table. Only hardwood should be used and it goes without saying that first one must ascertain that the wood is accurately machined so that the work resting on it will be at 90 degrees to the table.

Should it at any time be absolutely necessary to hold the work rather than clamping it, a

Work held in a drilling vice while being drilled. Sloppy work-holding techniques are very dangerous – always make sure that the work is held securely.

The component being drilled here would have had insufficient support from a drilling vice and so an additional heavy bar of metal has been clamped to it in order to give a greater holding area.

Because it was necessary to drill these three pieces accurately in line they were mounted in the vice together, but before doing so they were held together with double-sided adhesive tape to form them into one solid piece.

good stout glove should be worn on the hand used for holding the work. Even where full clamping is not possible and the work has to be hand-held, clamp some form of bar over the work that will act as a strap to prevent it rising up. It can be a piece of wood if suitable metal is not available. The main danger comes from the work starting to rotate with the machine, but it usually has to lift a little before it can start to rotate. To stop the rotational movement, fit some form of stop in a position that it will prevent the work rotating. A nut and bolt will

Although unable to get sufficient support with a drilling vice, this piece was made secure by clamping it to an angle plate, bolted to the drilling table.

Unable to fit these small pieces in a vice, they have been held to a piece of hardwood with screws.

The work is securely held but the drill too small to fit in the chuck, so first it has been put in a pin chuck and that is held in the machine.

do and the combination of the strap and the stop will ensure that the work, which will still be held in position by hand, will not cause any injury.

Countersinking

Countersinks are generally only required where it is necessary to mount a screw in a piece of work in such a way that the head of the screw lies flush or a little below the surface. A countersinking tool, however, is likely to be used far more for deburring holes rather than actually making countersinks, but whatever the use to which the tool is put it should be rotated at a slow speed and fed to the work at a very slow rate. Countersink tools come in a variety of sizes and are made with differing angles, as the heads on countersunk screws are also at varying angles. Most commonly, the angles associated with metalworking are 60 and 90 degrees. It is always difficult to avoid chatter when countersinking, no matter how securely the work is held, and the only remedy is to finish the countersink using a piece of emery

The photograph shows from left to right: a cone cut tool, used for making large diameter holes in sheet metal; two home-made counterbores; and a countersink tool.

cloth, on which the tool presses down during the final operation. This will give the appearance of a ground finish.

Counterboring

There are many occasions when the head of a screw or bolt, particularly a cap-head type of screw, needs to be recessed into the work. Unlike countersinking, the bottom of the recess is square and this operation is referred to as counterboring. A counterbore (the tool, not the work) is made with a pilot section to match the hole that is being dealt with, and attached to the shank immediately above the pilot is

---

Making a Counterbore

To make a counterbore, take a piece of silver steel of a slightly larger diameter than the bolt head or whatever the recess is to be for, then turn a short length to the diameter of the hole to be counter-bored to act as a pilot. Next, machine a suitable length to the required diameter; it will also be necessary to reduce a length to act as a shank as well. Mill or file two flats until they are in line with the pilot. Should they actually go slightly into the pilot it will not matter. Finally, shape the cutting edges as shown and then harden and temper the tool to a dark straw colour.

Right *A drawing showing how to make a counterbore.*

Sequence for making a counterbore
1 Machine pin for location
2 File or mill flats
3 Make cutting edges 10°
4 Harden and temper dark straw

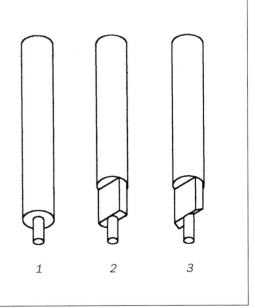

1   2   3

something like a small milling cutter that cuts into the metal. Although counterbores can be purchased, it is frequently difficult to find the exact size one requires and so generally it is far easier to make them as required.

'D' Bits

Another way of getting a suitable counterbore is first to drill out the length that has to be recessed and then to use a tool known as a 'D' bit to square it off at the base. 'D' bits can be obtained commercially, but the companies that stock them are few and far between and unless a full range is required it is not worth the bother of trying to source one as they are possibly the easiest tool there is to make.

An alternative method of making the 'D' bit is to grind a length of round high-speed steel into a 'D' bit, which will be far longer lasting than one made from silver steel. However, it needs a steady hand to make a nice job of it, as grinding a true flat is particularly difficult.

Reaming

Even the most carefully ground twist drill does not always produce a hole exactly to size and if

---

Making a 'D' Bit

Use a length of silver steel of the required diameter and file a short length of it flat to exactly half the diameter – the measurement is quite critical so check it with a micrometer. File an angle of about 10 degrees on the end to act as a cutting edge, harden and temper to dark straw colour, then finally just hone the edges with a small oilstone and the tool is ready for use.

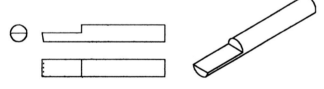

Construction of a "D" Bit
Used for squaring the bottom of blind holes, or as a reamer

How to make a 'D' bit.

A 'D' bit and above it a small taper reamer made by the same method.

one cutting edge should accidentally have been ground longer than the other, then the drill will definitely be cutting over size. The answer to this is to drill very slightly undersize and then ream the hole. A reamer consists of a tool with a number of flutes. Along the edge of each flute is a cutting edge and it is ground in manufacture to a very precise tolerance. To use a reamer it is simply necessary to drill the original hole about 0.2mm or $\frac{10}{1000}$in under size and rotate the reamer in it, while feeding it through. In the event of a reamer not being available for one reason or another, make a slight leading edge on a 'D' Bit and use that; it is surprising how accurate the results can be.

UNUSUAL SITUATIONS

From time to time, we come across components that are to be drilled and for one reason or another this cannot be done using normal methods. Here are a few ideas on how to cope with these situations.

Holes at Unusual Angles

If work is held at an angle in the machine vice there is a danger of it becoming unstable and pivoting when the pressure of the drill is applied. For this situation, an adjustable angle plate is used. The plate is set at the required angle using a protractor and the work or a vice is bolted to it. An adjustable angle plate can be made in the workshop, using two pieces of 12mm (0.5in) mild steel plate.

Drilling Through Round Bars

Drilling accurately through a round bar or tube can be a very difficult proposition, mainly because the original lining up of the drill over the centre is not accurate enough. For small work a simple jig such as that shown can be made. The jig is only suitable for small diameters. For larger material make a point on a short length of steel about 4mm diameter, place a short steel rule across the top of the work and bring the point to it. When it is central the rule will be perfectly level.

An adjustable angle plate can be used to support work for drilling at unusual angles. Set the plate with a protractor and clamp the work to it.

A simple idea for cross-drilling a small round bar or tube. It consists only of three flat strips made to pivot on two supporting bars with the locating hole placed centrally. Because the bars can swivel it is adaptable to a whole range of sizes.

The jig is too small to use on larger material; perfectly accurate location can be made using a pointed piece of steel and a steel rule.

A large diameter tube drilled accurately through the centre using the method shown.

Awkward Places

Frequently it is just impossible to get a drill into somewhere and even a long series will not do the job. By simply drilling a hole in a length of steel rod and securing the drill with a retaining compound a drill of any required length can be made.

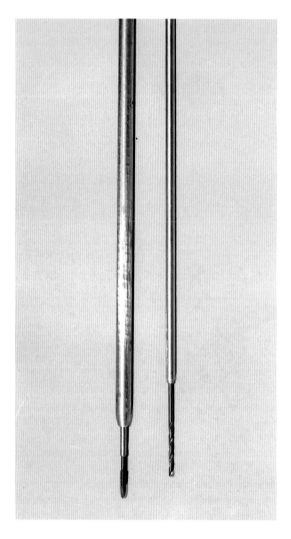

A drill extension made by securing a drill in a length of mild steel rod. Retaining compound holds it in place and gently heating the rod afterwards will enable it to be removed. The photograph shows a drill and tap dealt with in this way.

The extended drill in use making a hole to be tapped with the extended tap.

Another awkward situation that was dealt with by making a drill extension.

SAFETY

At all times it must be remembered that a drilling machine can be very dangerous and safety precautions should be taken when using one. A guard should be used on the actual machine and it is important that safety glasses are worn at all times. Certain materials will throw off fine particles of swarf that can be very hot and cause permanent eye damage. It is also essential to ensure that the machine is mounted on a firm, flat surface and if possible bolted to it in order to prevent it moving or toppling over during use. When picking up an object that has just been drilled, remember that it is likely to be hot enough to cause a nasty burn; it is best to leave it to cool before attempting to do so. There is also every chance that there will be ragged edges around the hole or holes that have been drilled and these are capable of causing very nasty cuts.

7 Bench Work

Separating one type of metalwork from another is very difficult because everything overlaps. Sheet metalworking, for example, includes the ability to cut metal as well as to file, finish and solder, but in particular it also includes the ability to bend and roll it to shape, and it is this aspect of things that this chapter will deal with.

HAND TOOLS

Hammers
For general-purpose work the metalworker uses only two types of hammer. They are known as a cross pein and ball pein; the latter is used for riveting. Unless one is engaged in heavy ironwork, a hammer is never used with any great force and so there is no need for a very heavy one. With use, the face will become pitted and marked and these marks will be transferred to the work and so it should occasionally be ground smooth.

Various types of hammers with soft faces are available and are useful where it is necessary to avoid marking work. They are all double-ended and various materials are used for the faces. In most instances the heads now are of some form of plastic, but it is possible to buy them with one face made from copper and the other made from hide. The hide face is particularly useful where the hammer is being used to adjust work in a milling vice for setting-up purposes.

Pliers
In general, pliers do not find many uses in metalworking. Although they are always useful to have around as an aid to gripping awkward items, they should be kept out of the way as their use can cause damage to metal surfaces that is difficult to remove. One exception to the rule is a type generally known as gas pliers that are used to hold items being heated and a good pair of these is worth investing in. While ordinary pliers will quickly rust and in no time deteriorate if used for this purpose, gas pliers do not experience these problems.

Spanners
Spanners will be needed, not only to make adjustments to machines, but no doubt from time to time in order to assemble work. Ring spanners are easily stored by the simple process of hanging them on a nail or hook on a wall or the edge of a shelf, but open-ended spanners will need to be kept in a shallow tray, either in the form of a drawer or a box

Adjustable spanners are not to be recommended, as they damage nuts. Spanners that are slightly larger than the width of the nut can also cause damage.

Tool for the Job

It is a very good idea to keep spanners that are used on particular machines near to those machines, even though this might mean that two or more of the same size of spanner is needed. It saves having to move from one machine to another to find the right size.

Right *A cross pein hammer.*

Below *A ball pein hammer. This particular tool has a fibreglass shaft as against the more traditional wooden type.*

Right *A hammer with plastic faces to the head. This type is useful for a variety of purposes when it is important not to mark the work. A variety of different materials is available as faces, some very soft and others harder and tougher.*

Allen Keys

Allen keys are frequently needed, as many machines are now adjusted with Allen screws. Although often purchased as sets, they can also be purchased separately and sometimes it is better to do so, as the sets do not necessarily cover the range that might be required. As with open-ended spanners, care must be taken to use the correct size for the job in order to prevent wear. Even so, after a period of time the edges will become rounded and the key less effective; good quality keys are hardened and less prone to this effect than cheaper versions made from mild steel. Keys can be shortened to remove the rounded-off section and thus given extra life. Once the plastic wallet has disintegrated or if they are bought individually, they can be stored in a block of hardwood with suitably sized holes to accept individual keys.

Handles for Allen Keys

It is possible to make handles for Allen keys that make them both easier to store and use. Simply drill a short length of mild steel in the lathe to the size across the flats of the key and cross-drill it to take a tommy bar. Grind the angled section off the Allen key, leaving a short pointed end, then gently hammer it into the hole in the bar. Finally secure the tommy bar.

Clamps

By far the most useful type of clamp is the toolmaker's, which is designed to apply pressure over an area, rather than in one place.

BENDING METAL

Many tasks that are undertaken will involve bending metal to various shapes. It might be a right-angled bend or possibly a particular angle will be called for; it is also possible that one might be called on to roll some sheet material. The amount of force needed to bend a piece of metal depends not only on how thick it is but also on its width. For example, a strip of metal 1.5mm thick and 25mm wide can easily be bent to a 90-degree angle in the vice, using nothing more that one's hands. Make that strip 50mm wide, and in all probability the task can no longer be accomplished. If it is 100mm in width then it will definitely be an impossibility to bend it without some aid. It is exactly the same thickness and so it is apparent that the force required is proportional to the width as well as the thickness. It also, of course, becomes more difficult as the metal gets thicker even if the width remains the same.

A useful hand clamp for bending very thin sheet metal.

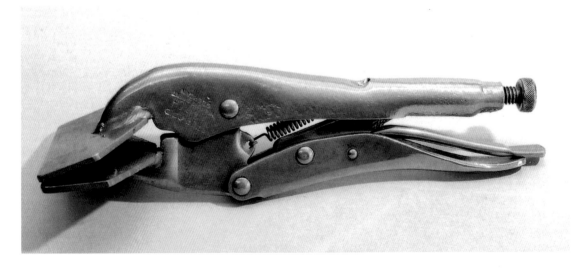

Making Toolmaker's Clamps

Toolmaker's clamps are easy to make – all that is needed are two lengths of square or rectangular bar and two set screws, which can be cap or hexagon headed. Stick the two pieces of bar together and drill and tap as shown in the drawing. Separate the two bars and fit the screws and there is the clamp. Although the clip shown on one of the screws makes for more convenience in use, the clamp will work perfectly well without it.

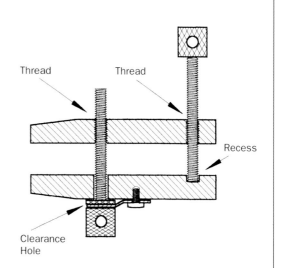

Right *A drawing showing the construction of a toolmaker's clamp. These are easily made in the workshop, frequently from little more than scrap material.*

Below *A photograph showing the versatility as well as the superb gripping power of the toolmaker's clamp.*

The use of a hammer can be quite effective, but unfortunately it does cause nasty marks in the metal and will not work very successfully on wide sheets, where the tendency is for the metal to bend in one area and not another, giving an uneven result. It may be a case of necessity that a hammer is used, and if so use one of the soft-faced variety, as at least it is less likely to leave

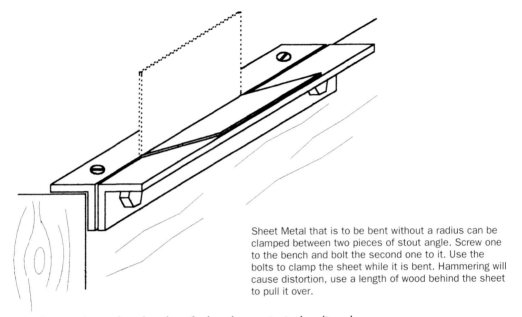

Sheet Metal that is to be bent without a radius can be clamped between two pieces of stout angle. Screw one to the bench and bolt the second one to it. Use the bolts to clamp the sheet while it is bent. Hammering will cause distortion, use a length of wood behind the sheet to pull it over.

Using an angle iron clamped to the edge of a bench to assist in bending sheet.

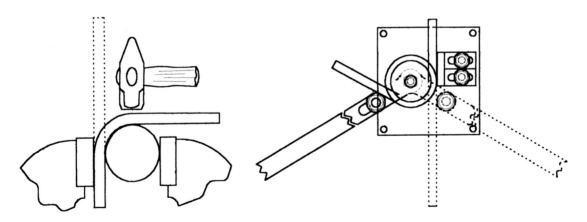

To bend bar to a radius in the vice clamp it together with a piece of bar of suitable diameter. If possible pull it round by hand. If not use a hammer, striking the blows as close to the securing jaw as possible.

A method of bending metal to a radius.

A simple home made bending jig. A handle is fitted under a roller of the required diameter and the metal held in place with angle iron. With good strong pivots and a long handle, metal up to 3mm thick can be bent.

A simple tool for bending strip to a radius, useful for decorative ironwork.

unsightly marks. Alternatively protect the piece that is being bent by holding another between that and the hammer. With thin sheet metal, by clamping it between two lengths of angle iron at either side of the joint it is possible to get a fairly even bend, but of course it will not be possible to take it over 90 degrees without releasing the angle irons.

JOINING METALS

We have four basic ways of joining metal sections together – they can be riveted; screwed or bolted; or joined by some means of soldering or welding; or stuck together, something that our grandfathers would have thought to be impossible.

RIVETING

Riveting is an art that has now largely disappeared from industry, modern techniques having made it obsolete. For the hobbyist, working in a small workshop at home, it is still one of the best ways of making a permanent joint between two pieces of metal. All it involves is drilling matching holes in two pieces of metal, inserting a rivet and then closing it up. The join is permanent as once rivets are properly closed they cannot come undone, although it is possible to remove them should it be necessary to do so at a later date.

Rivets

Rivets are made in iron, copper, brass and aluminium, and it is best to use those that match the job. They can have flat, countersunk, pan or round heads. The latter are called snap head and a specially shaped punch is used for closing them, not surprisingly referred to as a snap. No matter what shape the head is, prior to closing a drawing-down tool should be used to ensure that the rivet is pulled right home. The drawing-down tool is nothing more than a length of bar with a hole of the same diameter as the rivet shank. A ball pein hammer is used

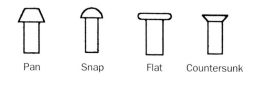

Rivet shapes.

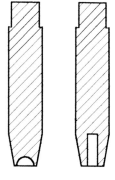

Sections through a snap dolly (left) and drawing down tool (right).

for riveting, the ball initially to shape the rivet as it is closed and the actual closing completed with a snap using the face of the hammer. All holes should be completely deburred before riveting takes place. Certain conventions should be observed, such as the proportions and spacing of the rivets, but apart from this it is a very simple process indeed. Generally, the diameter of rivet used will be the same as the thickness of a single plate that is being riveted, therefore if two plates 3mm thick are to be joined, a 3mm rivet is ideal. This cannot be a hard and fast rule, but is useful as a guide. The amount of a snap head rivet protruding above the plates when it is pushed home should be equal to one and a half times the diameter of its shank, and in the case of a countersunk one equal to the shank diameter. Rivets should be spaced at intervals equal to three times the shank diameter meter.

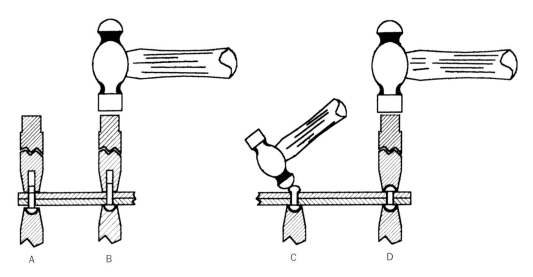

A Push drawing down tool over rivet shank
B Use drawing down tool to force rivet flush to plates
C Use pein of small hammer to shape rivet
D Use snap head dolly to fully close the rivet.

Note that the rivet head is throughout supported on a dolly held in a vice or supported on an anvil.

A sequence for closing snap head rivets.

SCREWING AND BOLTING

In some ways, there is a similarity between screwing or bolting two pieces of metal together and riveting, as both require matching holes to be drilled and the metal to be over-lapped. However, bolted joints are designed to be dismantled if required, while riveted ones are intended to be permanent. Bolting can also be used with thicker metal than riveting.

No matter how carefully one measures, there is still the possibility of slight errors when holes are drilled in two components with the intention that they are properly in line with each other. It is therefore a good idea when either riveting or bolting metal together, to first clamp the two parts together and drill through both at the same time. If this is done for rivets or for bolts that are to be secured on one side with nuts, it is no problem to drill through with the correct clearance-sized drill.

> ### Matching the Holes
>
> If the bolts are to be screwed into one of the layers of material the holes should be drilled the correct size for tapping, the pieces then separated and the holes in one piece opened to clearance size. The remaining piece is of course tapped.

There is no established standard for the size of bolts to be used when holding pieces together, and it is difficult to offer any real guidance other than to say that if one piece is to be tapped, the thread selected must be one that will give a minimum of four complete turns of the screw thread, and if possible six should be aimed for. When spacing bolts, have in mind that the strength of the joint will rely purely on the depth of the thread used, multiplied by the

116

Two plates to be joined by bolts. They are first clamped together and then both drilled at the same time. The plates shown are for a clock frame and as a high degree of accuracy was needed the holes were first reamed and then located with taper pins.

number of turns, and sufficient bolts need to be used to give the required strength.

If nuts are being fitted there should be at least one and a half turns of the thread visible after the nut has been fully tightened. Fitting a plain washer underneath the nut assists in tightening up by preventing the corners of the nut digging into the metal. If the component is likely to be subject to vibration, shake-proof washers should be used.

Bolts

Invariably, a workshop will contain a collection of various types of bolts, for which it is worth offering some description. Those referred to as screws will have heads that can be tightened with a screwdriver, they will possibly be cross head, rather than the more traditional slot. Sometimes a screw has a cap with a hexagon recess, which might be referred to as an Allen screw or cap screw and is used in conjunction

with an Allen key. The term bolt is generally applied to fixing devices that have a hexagon head, but there are two variations. A bolt will have a thread only part of its length, the section near the head being left as plain metal. If the thread extends the whole length it is described as a 'set', and if ordering bolts it is essential to specify whether it is bolts or sets that are wanted. These terms also apply to cap screws.

SOLDERING AND BRAZING

General Principles

All soldering is based on the same principle, the only differences being in the type of materials used. That principle is to raise the temperature of the work to the melting point of the material used for joining, which results in the joining material or solder adhering to the pieces that are being joined. As soon as any metal is heated,

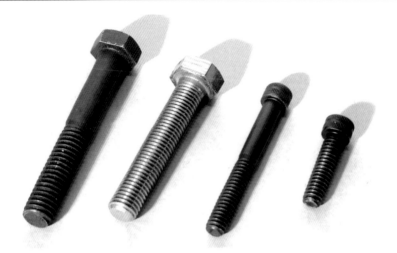

From left to right: a hexagon headed bolt; a hexagon headed set; a cap bolt and a cap set.

oxide forms on the surface and prevents solder from sticking to it. The formation of the oxide is the result of exposure of the hot metal to air and to counteract this a flux is used. Theoretically this can be anything that will exclude air, but in practice it is usual to use a purpose-made flux. The metal must always be thoroughly cleaned before soldering commences and a small amount of flux applied before heating. Some of the patent fluxes are reputed to clean off oxides while the metal is being heated and can be applied during the heating process. In all cases where a solder joint is to be made care must be taken not to overheat the metal, as doing so results in the destruction of the flux and in turn the formation of oxide, resulting in a bad joint.

Soft Soldering

Soft solders are alloys of tin and generally flow at temperatures ranging from about 150 to 250°C. They are suitable for soldering mild steel as well as non-ferrous metals. Soft solders are not as strong as harder silver solders, but because they melt at a much lower temperature they are easier to use. The lower temperature also means that it is possible to use soft solder with a soldering iron as well as with a small blowlamp. The quantity of metal contained in the project will be the deciding factor as to how much heat is required and therefore whether or not an iron can be used. Although it is generally best to apply flux to the joint before heating, some soft solders are available that have a flux core and are designed for use without pre-fluxing These solders melt at very low temperatures and have a very low strength.

Soldering Irons

Most soldering irons are heated by electricity, and are made in a wide range of sizes. As the amount of heat generated depends on the wattage of the iron, someone involved in making electronic equipment will need something very much smaller than a person who is making an item such as a copper kettle. Irons are available 15W to 150W, so it is possible to get one for almost any purpose.

The function of the iron is to heat the metal to which it is applied, until it reaches a temperature at which the solder will melt – unless the metal reaches that heat, a good joint cannot be made. All too frequently blobs of solder are applied by putting the solder on the iron, when the metal itself is nowhere near the right temperature. Deceptively, this will give a result that at a quick glance appears to be a good solder joint. However, more often than not this is not the case, and it is what is known as a dry joint, the solder having just about adhered to the metal but without any strength. It is possible to get soldering irons that are attached to gas torches and these are used in exactly the same way as one powered by electricity.

Using an Iron

The bit of an iron is the copper segment at the end that gets hot and this should always be kept clean and tinned. Tinning is the process of putting a thin layer of solder on the metal; it should be a fine coating with no blobs. The best way to clean and tin the iron is to run a smooth file over it until the copper is visible, then heat it until it is thought to be about the correct temperature to melt the solder. At this point, coat it with flux, afterwards applying a coating of solder. If the solder is too thick, wipe it over with a piece of felt while it is still hot. In use, the iron should be held in contact with both pieces of metal and solder applied to the metal as close to the tip as possible. Once the solder melts on the metal it can be run along the joint

by slowly drawing the iron along. The tinning of the iron attracts the solder to it, thus transferring it along the joint.

Fluxes

Various types of flux are available for soft soldering and it is largely a matter of personal preference as to which one is used. In liquid form and sold under various trade names is Spirits of Salts, a mildly corrosive acid that is particularly useful when soldering steel. At one time little else would have been used for that sort of work. Other fluxes come in the form of a paste or a gel and have various materials as a base; some use resin and others tallow, both of which are old and tried flux materials.

Small Blowlamps

A tiny gas blowlamp can be used for soft soldering, the principle being much the same as when an iron is used, except that instead of the

A tiny gas blowlamp, which is suitable for small work. Although the temperature at the tip of the flame reaches over 1,000°C, there is little volume and the temperature rapidly disperses.

The blowlamp in use. The two pieces of metal being joined have been wired together with iron wire that has deliberately been allowed to get dirty in order that the solder will not stick to that as well as the job.

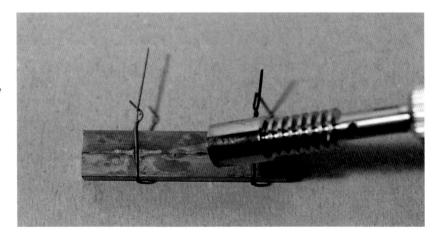

tip drawing the solder along the joint, the flame of the lamp is moved and followed with additional solder. The result is usually a joint with more solder residue than when an iron is used, although it does not follow that the joint is any stronger.

Hard Solders

There is frequently some confusion between silver soldering and brazing, which is hardly surprising as apart from the materials both are identical. Silver soldering, or as it is sometimes called, silver brazing, involves the use of alloys with silver content as the joining material, whereas in brazing the joining material is known as spelter and is brass rod with a comparatively low melting point. There is a wide range of silver solders, ranging between melting points of approximately 600°C to 900°C.

Borax Fluxes

Whether brazing or silver soldering, the flux will be based on Borax. Although manufacturers mix it with other chemicals, ordinary household Borax can safely be used. Generally, the flux in powder form is mixed with water plus a little washing-up liquid and applied as a paste. An additional amount can be introduced by slightly heating the rod and dipping it in the powder, which will then adhere to it. Frequently, the water that has been used to mix the flux will boil as the metal heats up, causing the flux to run into areas where it is not required. In turn, the solder will follow it, leaving a nasty and unwanted mess on the work. Some sort of control can be achieved by drawing a line with a pencil round the joint, about 3mm away from it, which will prevent it running. Another method is to mix the flux with methylated spirits, which will evaporate as the metal is heated, leaving the flux in the required place.

Problems with Fumes

Whether soft or hard soldering, there is a danger if the fumes that are created should be breathed in. While they are unlikely to prove fatal, they can cause a sore throat and discomfort to the eyes. They will also create deep, penetrating rust on any nearby tools. Soldering therefore is best carried out in a special area of the workshop, where there is plenty of ventilation.

A blowlamp used with propane and oxygen, giving sufficient heat to allow brazing.

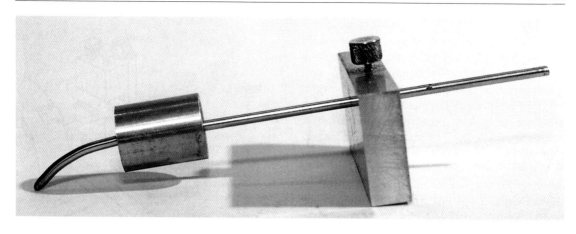

A simple but very efficient home-made clamp for holding sheet metal in place while soldering or brazing. The probe rests on the sheet and the weight is adjusted by moving the cylinder or base.

Soldering Aluminium

Aluminium oxidizes very quickly indeed and is therefore extremely difficult to solder, but there are a couple of techniques that can be successful. The first and most useful one is to use a small stainless steel wire brush and a length of thin stainless steel rod filed to a point. The metal is cleaned with the brush, then both parts are heated simultaneously a little way from the where the joint is to be. The heat flows to where it is needed and while this is happening the metal is cleaned by scratching it with the stainless steel rod; aluminium solder is applied immediately before oxidization can start. No flux is needed because there is no opportunity for the metal to oxidize.

WELDING

Whereas a solder or brazing joint relies on the solder adhering to both of the parts in order to join them together, welding is the action of fusing them together by melting them. The old-time blacksmith used to weld by literally putting the pieces in a furnace, and just as they were about to reach melting point hammering them together. These days, welds are made either by heating the metal with a mixture of gas and oxygen, or by using a very high-powered electric current to create sufficient heat to do the job, or a mixture of gas and electric current. In each case, although the joint relies on the molten state of the parts, another metal is introduced to act as a filler. A gap the width of about half the thickness of the material being welded should be left between the parts being joined, and the molten metal allowed to flow from one to the other. It is important to remember that the welding rod is only used as filler and not to try and use it as a form of solder.

Gas Welding

Gas welding is usually carried out with a mixture of acetylene and oxygen or occasionally propane and oxygen. The heat of the flame will depend to a large extent on the quantity of oxygen and is kept moving across the components being joined until the metal is seen to melt and form a small pool of molten metal,

---

Fittings

When using acetylene gas, fittings must not be made of copper or alloys containing copper. This is because when exposed to the action of acetylene, copper forms a highly explosive compound called copper acetylide that is easily detonated by heat or friction.

---

at which point the filler metal is introduced. No flux is needed and although the filler rod does have a coating that helps to clean the metal, in general so much heat is generated that the flame is self-cleaning. Special coloured welding goggles should always be worn for gas welding and thick gloves are also advisable.

Arc Welding

Arc welding is less popular than it used to be. It relies on a transformer supplying a very heavy current – on one side of the circuit is an electrode into which is fitted the filler rod that is coated with a form of flux; the other side is secured to the work with a very heavy clamp. As the electrode is brought close to the work, a spark is created that generates the heat to melt the metal. This must be kept at a small distance from the work, because if it touches it a short circuit will occur and the spark ceases. The art is to move the electrode along the joint at a set distance in order to keep the weld smooth.

The sparks created by arc welding can cause serious damage to the eyes and so a special shield must be used for protection. It is also essential to wear heavy protective gloves to prevent burns from falling sparks that contain minute quantities of red-hot metal. A particular problem caused by looking directly at the sparks is called arc-eyes, which is very painful and can cause temporary blindness; medical help should be sought at once if pain in the eyes is felt.

Welding with Inert Gases

Gas or arc welding are fine on mild or carbon steel, but of no use when welding stainless steel or aluminium, because of the problem of oxidization. The system used to weld these metals is to weld through a thin film of an inert gas that will prevent oxides from forming; generally the gas will be Argon. Various welding sets are sold that will do this sort of job and they are usually described by a series of initials such as Mig or Tig, the 'ig' standing for inert gas, and the first initial for the type of electrode that is used.

ADHESIVES AND FILLERS

At one time, adhesives played virtually no part whatever in metalworking operations, as there were no suitable substances available. The only type of adhesive that might be used was a form of tarry substance, applied hot to secure small work to a lathe face plate, or some similar operation. The chemical industry spent many years developing different types of adhesives. Possibly the first major example of their use was during World War II, when the famous Mosquito aircraft was largely held together with epoxy resin. The range of adhesives is now very wide and as well as there being a number of different types of substance, there are also variations on each type, therefore for the best results it is as well to know the type to use as well as how to use it.

Although different types of adhesive require different techniques that will be mentioned when that type is dealt with, there are a couple of basic rules that apply to them all. Firstly, with very few specific exceptions both parts of the work must be clean and free from grease. The best thing for removing grease completely is washing-up liquid. Methylated spirits, petrol and cellulose thinners are also excellent and will remove every particle of oil or grease. White spirit is not suitable because although it does remove heavy grease deposits, it is in itself oil-based and will leave a smear of oil that is not detectable to the naked eye. There must be sufficient area of metal for the adhesive to be able to grip if it is to be effective, therefore it is not possible to butt two pieces of sheet metal on end. All adhesives work on the principle of air exclusion, and so every effort must be made to ensure that the parts to be secured are flat and flush with each other.

Basic glues can play a small part in metalworking. For example, if a complicated part is to be cut from sheet metal it may sometimes be possible to stick a paper pattern to the metal and use it as a template cutting. The glue must be water-soluble so that it can washed off when the work is completed. For

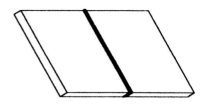

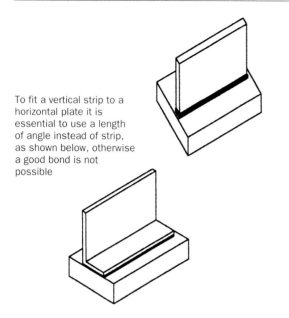

To fit a vertical strip to a horizontal plate it is essential to use a length of angle instead of strip, as shown below, otherwise a good bond is not possible

It is not possible to join two plates, side by side. A butt strip must be fitted as shown below

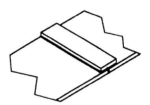

The drawing shows good and bad ways of using adhesives. The two views at the top will have no strength at all. Those at the bottom will be quite strong.

more robust work, impact adhesives can be used. Both pieces to be joined are covered and the adhesive allowed to dry, or nearly dry. The parts are then brought together and will form a very strong bond. It is particularly useful where rubber or plastic components need to be stuck to metal, an obvious example being protective strips or feet.

Cyanoacrylate Adhesives

From the simple basic sticky stuff we can move on to the so-called 'super glues'. These are cyanoacrylate adhesives and while most people are quite familiar with them, it is at this stage that we start to see the wide variations that are available. Normal super glue as sold in supermarkets is useful for household purposes, but generally speaking it is not for us. These adhesives are available in various strengths, fluidity and drying times. Super glues do have some uses for the metalworker, however, in that they are useful for holding small parts together while working on them and can even be used for securing work to a milling table or lathe faceplate while machining operations are carried out. The adhesive has little shear strength and when the job is complete a sharp tap with a mallet will as a rule be sufficient to separate the parts; if that fails, it is possible to obtain special debonding agents for separating the pieces. As super glues are particularly adept at sticking flesh together it is essential to take great care in their use; should this accidentally happen, soak the hands in hot water to which a little washing-up liquid has been added. A more recent development in the field of cyanoacrylate adhesives has been to incorporate rubber fibres within, giving a vastly increased strength.

Anaeroboric Adhesives

Like the cyanoacrylates, this type of adhesive comes in a variety of strengths designed for various purposes. Generally, the name will give an idea of the strength – screwlocking, nutlocking, studlocking and retaining speak for themselves. Even the individual types have differing strengths and so if we were to purchase a screwlocking type it would be necessary to obtain one suitable for the type of thread on which it is to be used. If working in very fine materials and using say 1.4mm thread, the weakest solution would be needed, while obviously for a 25mm thread it would be necessary to use a much stronger one. Whatever the thread, the technique for the use of the adhesive is the same – it should be applied to the male portion and not dropped in the hole, and only sufficient to cover a length of one and a half times the thread diameter should be used. Apart from the ability to prevent a thread from coming undone in use, there is an additional advantage as the material also prevents corrosion setting in, thus ensuring that with a little pressure the thread can always be undone and it is unlikely for the screw to break in the hole because of corrosion. It is possible to use a drop of paint on a thread to prevent it from releasing itself and this can be a good short-term cure; however, after a period of time the paint becomes brittle and is no longer effective. The other versions of the anaeroboric adhesives relate almost entirely to the varying strengths needed for the different tasks and application is the same. It is necessary to allow a small gap for the adhesive to do its work, the size of which is usually stipulated on the container; it is generally in the region of one-hundredth of a millimetre. The retaining compounds are used for very high strength work. They are not suitable for sticking flat surfaces together, only for securing pieces in mating holes. In the event of it being necessary to release parts secured with the adhesive, the application of a small amount of heat will do the job.

Sealing

There are various sealing compounds, designed to be used as gaskets, pipe sealers and so on. Again, there is a wide variety. Most of the pipe-sealing compounds are designed for use before assembly; however, it is possible to obtain some that can be used afterwards. Some of these sealants are designed with sufficient strength to

allow their use on hydraulic fittings. It is desirable that most pipe sealants and gaskets are given sufficient time after application to cure before being taken into service.

Gluing Flat Surfaces

There are two types of adhesive suitable for joining flat surfaces; they are epoxy resins and acrylates. The epoxy resin comes in two parts, the adhesive and a hardener, which are usually mixed in equal quantities and then applied to the work. They are available as either normal or quick-drying types, with the normal taking about twenty-four hours to cure, while the rapid action one takes between two to four hours. Some variation in the drying time of either type can be obtained by mixing a slightly greater or lesser quantity of hardener, but the more hardener, the weaker the bond. Generally speaking, the standard type has greater strength than the quick-drying version, and both will cure more rapidly if gentle heat is applied. Acrylate adhesives also come in two parts, but as a resin adhesive and a liquid hardener. The adhesive is applied to one surface and the hardener to the other, the parts are then brought together and curing is reasonably quick. The adhesive is more tolerant of slightly greasy surfaces than others and is now used in industry in many instances where at one time spot welding would have been required.

A most unlikely material that can be of a great deal of use to the metalworker is double-sided sticky tape, particularly the type usually sold for sticking carpets to the floor. It can be used to hold work on the lathe faceplate, the milling table and drilling machine table. Once secured, the work can be drilled, filed, sawn, milled or turned with success, although removing the tape afterwards can be a little difficult because the bond is so good and it might be necessary to soak everything in white spirit until it releases. In spite of this, it is an ideal way of holding work when it is impossible to secure it with clamps.

8 The Lathe

Most metalworkers will need a lathe, which is the most versatile of any machine. Not only can it be used for turning, but it is also capable of milling and drilling and there are numerous instances where people have customized their machine in order to use them for special jobs for which they were never intended in the first place. Lathes have been in use for over a thousand years, and although modern machines are very different from the early ones the principle of their construction has remained the same, with modifications taking place very slowly indeed.

BUYING A LATHE

There is now a wide choice when buying a lathe. Not so many years ago, the prospective purchaser had little choice but to buy a second-hand model, but there are now numerous cheap machines imported from the Far East. This does not mean that the used market should be ignored, as there is plenty of choice there as well. It is necessary to have some idea of what to look for, whether buying new or otherwise, and obviously this becomes more important when the lathe has been in use and might have been badly treated by its previous owner or owners.

Sizes

There is a wide range of sizes, from tiny ones, made with watchmakers in mind, to enormous machines capable of machining very large diameters. The sizes are quoted in two ways: centre height, which is the distance between the exact centre of the mandrel and the lathe bed; and the distance between centres, which as it implies is the distance between a centre fitted in the mandrel and one fitted in the tailstock. Sometimes the height of the centre in relation to the cross slide and the height over the gap will also be quoted. The latter refers to the fact that some lathes have a gap in front of the headstock, giving an increase in height for a limited length.

The selection of size will depend on two factors – the type of work it will be used for and the amount of space available in the workshop. The most popular size for a home workshop is a centre height of about 85mm (3.5in). The person who is only going to make clocks, small models, jewellery and so on, will want a small machine and should look for one with a height above centres of about 50mm (2in). If heavier work is involved a larger machine becomes a necessity, but as a large machine does not cope very well with small work it is not unusual for people to have a small lathe as well as a large one.

Buying a Used Lathe

The usual advice given to those wishing to buy a used lathe is to take somebody with them who knows a lot about machines, although that is not always possible. Fortunately, even if one has no knowledge at all it is not too difficult to get some idea of how good the machine is likely to be. Start by establishing the make of the lathe and then go along to the local library. Ask to

An older type of lathe but in excellent condition, that one might be able to find on the used machine market.

look at a copy of *The Machinist's Handbook*, and find out from that whether or not it is a well-known make. Shortly after World War II a large number of machines were made in engineering factories that had no other work. These were quite good machines, but if spares should be needed they will be impossible to get. While this would not worry a skilled machinist who would be able to make any part required, it could prove a disaster for someone with limited ability. Therefore it is best to go for a well-known make, preferably one that is still in production or where a supplier of parts is listed in the handbook, unless you have confidence in your ability to cope with any repairs that might be needed.

Look at the machine carefully and ask yourself the following questions. Is the bed in good condition, or has it been damaged in any way? Is the overall condition of the machine good, or are the castings chipped and battered?

Has it been repainted, if so was it painted just to keep the machine in good condition, or has the paint been used to cover up cracks in the castings? Is it complete with chucks, tool post, tailstock, and so on? If the answer to all these questions is in the affirmative, check the saddle to see how much backlash there is on the handle and whether there is any unwanted movement when shaken. (Backlash is the amount of rotation of the handle before the saddle starts to move along the bed and a small amount is inevitable but it should be no more than one-eighth of a turn of the handle at the very most.) Check that when the slide is wound along there are no places where a sudden jerk is felt that might indicate some damage.

Checking the Headstock

A simple test for wear in the headstock bearings is to fit the faceplate, put a length of wood underneath to act as a lever and see if the mandrel moves. If it is possible to do so, fit up a clock gauge so that the amount of movement can be measured. Many lathes have metal shims in the headstocks that can be taken out to adjust the bearings and some movement might not indicate a complete disaster, but it is worth finding out whether there is any adjustment available. See the lathe in operation and listen to the sound it makes, the bearings should make a smooth purring sound. If there is an uneven noise or loud rumblings, they are probably damaged. Finally, run a finger in the mandrel bore. All lathes have a taper in the bore to accept tools – establish that this taper is not scored in any way and do the same to the one that is in the tailstock. A scored taper can reduce the accuracy of the lathe, so if the mandrel taper feels rough in any way ask to see the lathe in operation with a centre in the bore and check that the centre runs true.

A nice medium-sized lathe, the EMCO Compact 5 is ideal for the home workshop. It is seen here in a warehouse specializing in machine tools and where expert advice is available.

Buying a New Lathe

The best advice that can be given to someone buying a new lathe is to go to a specialist that deals in workshop machinery rather than the local DIY store or car accessory warehouse. A specialist dealer will be better able to offer advice on the most suitable machine for your particular needs and should have machines available for demonstration, which the would-be purchaser should be allowed to operate. There will be an after-sales service and as a rule advice will be available by telephone if it is needed. Most specialist dealers will not only deliver the machine, but will also be prepared to set it up as well. Visit one or two of the many exhibitions that are staged throughout the year, whether devoted to machinery or aimed at model engineers. In either instance, there will be a range of machines on sale, some of which can be tried out, and more often than not there are demonstrations of machining techniques.

LATHE EQUIPMENT

The amount of equipment, tools, gadgets and so on that will eventually be acquired and will enable the machine to carry out the many functions it is capable of will be built up over a period of time, but when buying a lathe it is wise to ensure that a certain amount of equipment comes with it. The minimum requirement should be two centres, a faceplate, a chuck and a tailstock chuck, and if only one chuck is part of the package make sure it is a four-jaw independent type. A three-jaw self-centring chuck is of little use on its own, as the only material it will accept is round or hexagonal bar stock, which limits the lathe to machining that type of material. It has been known for lathes to be sold by non-specialist stores with only a three-jaw self-centring chuck for work-holding and no other work-holding equipment available for the machine. Such a machine will be a complete waste of money.

A really top quality lathe, the Maximat Super, which is built to very high standards.

Chucks

Chucks are generally available in three forms: three-jaw self-centring; four-jaw self-centring and four-jaw with independently operating jaws. In the case of self-centring chucks it is usual for two sets of jaws to be supplied, described as inside and outside. This is a rather loose description meaning that with the inside type work is always held in the middle of the jaws as they close, whereas with the outside type work can be held on the steps of the jaws, but as a rule not held in the middle. Four-jaw independent chucks invariably have jaws that are reversible and can be used either way round, and as an added bonus when irregular-shaped work is being held it is possible to use any combination of inside or outside. Usually a chuck will be fitted to a back plate that has a

The four-jaw chuck is very adaptable and will hold a variety of odd shapes, such as this one which is in the process of being set up.

fitting to suit the lathe mandrel, and it goes without saying that the accuracy with which the back plate is fitted will control that accuracy of the chuck. In the case of a lathe that has a threaded mandrel for holding the chuck it is sometimes possible to purchase one that will screw directly in place, this not only means greater accuracy but also brings the chuck closer to the headstock so that if the lathe has a gap bed there is more room in which to work.

Adjusting a Four-Jaw Chuck

Many people find this type of chuck difficult to work with because of the need to adjust work to run true. However, it is not such a hard task as might be expected, and as the other types of chuck never run absolutely true it is well worth teaching oneself to adjust the four-jaw chuck

correctly. Start by marking a point on the work which will be the centre of any turning operations, and then put the work in the chuck so that the mark is as near as possible in line with the tailstock centre. Tighten the jaws to hold the work, but do not at that point tighten them hard enough to grip the work during operations. Then rotate the lathe by hand; it is most unlikely that the work will run true. Move it round so that the wide part of the eccentric circle it forms is at the rear, very slightly loosen the nearest jaw and tighten the one furthest away and make a further check, repeating the operation until it is rotating accurately. Then tighten the jaws in strict rotation sufficiently to hold the work for machining operations to commence. When adjusting round bar in the four-jaw chuck it may be necessary to loosen two jaws, to allow sufficient clearance for the metal to be moved. It is a process that improves with practice and absolute accuracy can then be achieved. To keep moving the key from one jaw to another can be time-consuming and it is a good idea to make special small keys for adjusting purposes.

Soft Jaws

The jaws of lathe chucks are very hard. They are made that way as during their lifetime they will be put under a great deal of pressure and will be continually moved. For most work this does not matter, but sometimes the hardness of the jaw can create unwanted marks or even indentations in the work and so a softer surface will be required. Special soft jaws can be bought that are used to replace the normal jaws when required.

Instead of using soft jaws, it is sometimes possible to insert shims between the jaws and work. This can also be done with a four-jaw independent chuck, although in that case they are likely to fall out when adjustments are made and it is worth considering sticking them in place with a quick-setting adhesive that can be removed when the job in hand has been completed. It is also possible to make soft jaws for oneself by simply boring pieces of suitable bar material and securing them to the jaws of the chuck with grub screws.

The Faceplate

Before the chuck was invented all work that could not be supported between centres was done on a faceplate, and although these days many people seem to fight shy of their use they are easily the most versatile method there is of

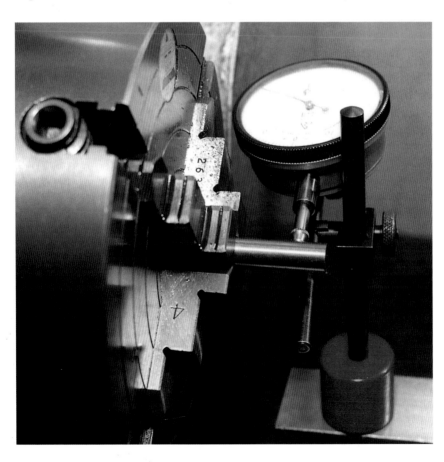

For final accuracy when setting up work in a four-jaw chuck use a clock gauge.

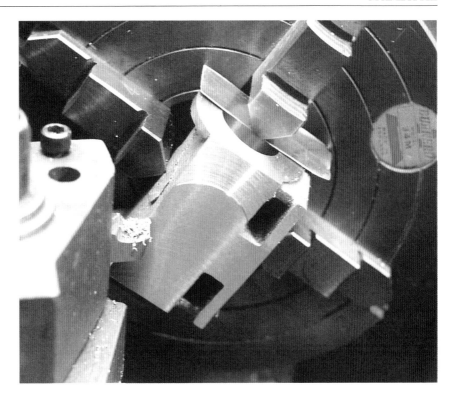

Shims inserted between the chuck jaws and work will protect the work from damage caused by the hard jaws.

Work bolted to the faceplate. In this case, additional security is obtained by using a device known as a Keats Angle Plate.

holding work. As the faceplate will usually be used for heavy work, it follows that machining speeds will generally be low and a lot of torque will be created. It is therefore essential that work is clamped very securely to the plate and a minimum of three clamping points used. Should the shape of the work make it impossible to use three points, two will have to suffice, but the clamps in that case should be as wide as possible to ensure that the work is held securely. Never use a single clamp.

Working Between Centres

The most accurate way of working with round bars is to support them between centres, which involves using two centres, a soft one in the mandrel and a hard or rotating one in the tailstock. A bracket known as a driving dog is fitted to the work at the mandrel end and driven by a driving plate, which is rather like a faceplate without slots and with a peg sticking out. As the lathe rotates this catches the driving dog and rotates the work. In this way, the accuracy of the lathe itself is in use and there are no discrepancies caused by an inaccurate chuck. It is essential to keep the support at the tailstock well greased so as to reduce wear and prevent overheating.

Collets

Collets are small chucks that will only hold one size of metal. They slip straight into the mandrel and are generally tightened with a nose cap. This means that the structure of the lathe is used, without the problems that can be created by a chuck, and as a result holding work in collets results in a very high degree of accuracy.

Using a Centre Lathe

The basic operation of a lathe is quite easy. Work is held on the mandrel by one means or another and a cutting tool is moved along the bed via the saddle; it is brought into contact with the metal, some of which is removed. If it is necessary to drill a hole, a drill can be put in the tailstock chuck and wound in to the work.

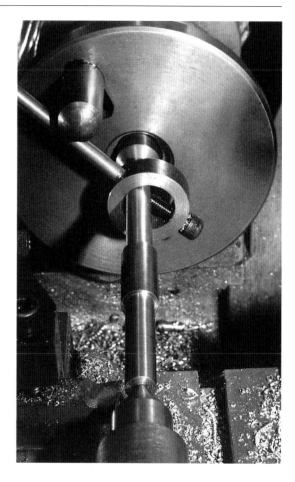

Machining between centres. The work is supported between the headstock and tailstock on centres and rotated by a driving dog.

Cutting Tools

Most tools used for general work on a lathe are nothing more than a short length of special steel, ground to a particular profile to enable them to complete particular operations. It is necessary to grind the cutting edges of tools to various angles that allow not only for cutting, but also for strength. The chart on page 134 shows this far better than it could ever be explained in words. While it is nice to get the angles right, it will not be the end of the world if they are a degree or two out. To some extent tool angles can be varied according to the job in hand, something that cannot be reflected in the

Effects of tool height positioning

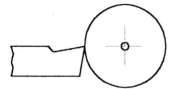 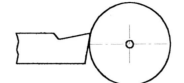 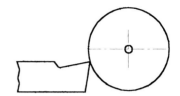

Tool at exact centre height giving correct clearance angles

Cutting edge above centre height, reducing clearance angle and causing tool to rub rather than cut.

Cutting edge below centre height, increasing clearance angle and so weakening tool, which tends to slip under the work and create bad finish

Tool shapes and their uses

Tool for fine finishing, note small radius for smooth cut

Knife edge tool has sharp corner for facing off square

Roughing tool round cutting edge helps when taking heavy cuts

Round nose tool also used for heavy cuts as well as for making grooves

Screw cutting tool angle is ground to suit thread and tip is radiused also to suit thread

Form tool, made to a specific shape. The tool is best made from carbon steel in order that radii can be machined with an end mill, etc.

Chart showing shapes of lathe tools and the purposes for which they are used.

chart. The angles that are shown give the best results and have been formulated to enable swarf to clear quickly, and as far as possible to stop heat building up along the cutting edges of the tool. It is therefore possible when machining very small diameters to increase the angle of the cutting edge as less heat will then build up; the steeper angle will also allow more rapid removal of swarf.

TIPPED TOOLS

Brazed Tips

Tools with special cutting tips are now highly popular. The tip may be made of a variety of materials, the most common being tungsten. Tips may be either brazed to a shaft or screwed into place, in which case they are replaceable; in either instance a wide range of different types can be obtained. Because the material is so hard it wears better and therefore the tool needs to be sharpened less often. Where a tool has a brazed tip, it can only be sharpened with the use of a special grindstone that is coloured green, and honing must be done with a diamond lap. The shape of the tool does not differ in any way from the standard type of lathe tool, except that the tip is brazed in place in such a way as to stand proud of the body. Tipped tools are often sold as sets that contain several different shapes, but buying them this way is a bit of a waste as it will often be found that two or three only will be used, the others being of shapes that will find no use in the average workshop.

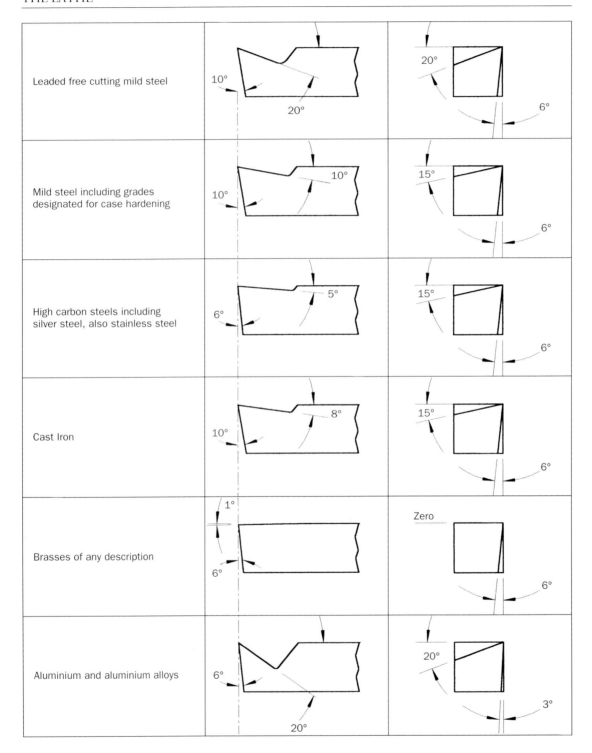

Leaded free cutting mild steel		
Mild steel including grades designated for case hardening		
High carbon steels including silver steel, also stainless steel		
Cast Iron		
Brasses of any description		
Aluminium and aluminium alloys		

Chart showing cutting and clearance angles of lathe tools for various metals.

Replaceable Tips

Tools with replaceable tips are only obtainable as individual items and have a number of advantages. For example, it is possible to purchase tips of various qualities, designed especially for different metals as well as for rough machining and fine finishing. In addition, if a tip does break during operations a new one can be quickly screwed into place without any loss of the setting position. Unfortunately, both tips and holders are rather expensive but it is possible to make the holders for oneself, from mild steel bar, by simply milling a suitable recess to accept the tip, then drilling and tapping a hole to allow it to be screwed up tight. Some care is necessary when milling the recess, as it is essential that the support platform for the tip is absolutely flat, otherwise there is a danger of it breaking.

All tipped tools, whether with interchangeable tips or those that are brazed on, are very brittle and prone to chipping and so are not suitable for interrupted work, which generally rules out their use on castings, particularly those made of iron. Apart from this, the tools have many advantages. For example, because they are less affected by heat it is unnecessary to use any cooling liquids with them and cutting speeds can be considerably higher than with normal high-speed tools. The high cutting speed generally means that the finish on the metal being machined will be of a higher quality than if a non-tipped tool is used.

Tool Height

It is essential that any turning tool is mounted in the tool post in such a way that the cutting tip is exactly at centre height, that is, the height of the centre point of the mandrel. Unless the height setting is correct a good result will never be achieved. If the cutting edge is too low the work will tend to ride over it and if it is too high, the body of the tool will be rubbing instead of cutting. The tool height can be set by comparing it with a centre set in the tailstock.

Machining Operations

Two more very important things to remember when turning, in addition to the necessity to have the cutting edge of the tool at centre height, is to always work as close to the chuck as possible and to have the cutting tool supported as near to the cutting edge as possible. Undue overhang in either of these places will result in chatter and consequently a bad finish to the work. Also it is necessary to ensure that the lathe is running at the correct speed for the work and to use a cutting fluid if necessary. The traverse must not be too fast, and the slower the tool is moved along the work the better the quality of the finish. The formula for working out the correct rotational speed for machining is complicated by the fact that there are so many different types of metal, requiring different speeds. It is best to work on the principle that the larger the work diameter and the harder the metal, the slower the lathe should rotate.

A tool with a replaceable tungsten tip.

135

Whether or not the auto-feed is used for traversing the tool is a matter of personal choice. For some people it is the only way to obtain an even movement, while others find they can work better by hand. Unless it is intended to machine a component to an angle, the saddle should always be used for all operations and the top slide should only be used for making short angles. If it is necessary to machine work that has to be some distance from the headstock, it should be supported with a centre held in the tailstock and a steady placed as near as possible to where the work is being done. There are two main types of steady: fixed one which is bolted to the lathe bed and has three points to support the work; and a travelling type that bolts to the saddle and has two support points, one immediately above the cutting tool and the other opposite it. For very small diameter work it is usual to use a type of steady with a bush that is specially made to accept the work.

A steady for small work, which is bolted to the saddle. Prior to starting work, a brass or nylon bush is inserted in the hole and held in place with a screw. It is drilled to the same diameter as the workpiece, using a drill in the headstock.

Work supported by a three-point steady.

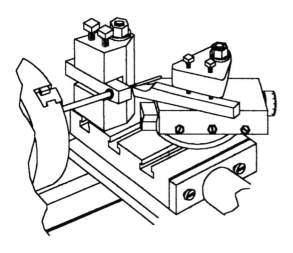

A bar of metal in the rear tool post used as a steady for small work, a set-up that allows machining to take place very close to the steady and is particularly useful when machining small tapers.

Drilling

Holes can be made by drilling or boring, depending on the diameter and possibly the type of hole required as well. For example, it might be stepped or it could be blind, with maybe a particular angle needed at the bottom. A start should always be made with a centre drill of an appropriate size and when the drill is taken into use it should be constantly withdrawn to allow swarf to clear. If appropriate, a cutting fluid should be used and the machine should be run at the correct speed for the type of material being drilled. Most tailstocks have some means of measuring the depth to which a drill will have penetrated the work. However, as a rule the graduations are rather on the coarse side and it may be necessary use a depth gauge.

Boring

Boring is done with a small cutting tool on an extended arm. Like ordinary cutting tools,

A chart on the headstock of the Cowells Lathe conveniently gives settings for spindle speeds.

COWELLS MODEL 90 ME					
SPEED RANGE 1	HEADSTOCK PULLEY				
	BACK GEARED	60	110	180	
	DIRECT DRIVE	280	500	880	
SPEED RANGE 2	BACK GEARED	140	240	440	
	DIRECT DRIVE	640	1130	2100	

Left *A boring bar being used to machine a large diameter hole in a part for a model steam engine.*

Below *An awkward casting mounted on the lathe saddle for boring between centres. Note the boring bar is mounted between centres for accuracy.*

Boring Long Holes

When very long holes are being bored there may be a chance that the boring bar will flex a little and so it is advisable when making the finishing cuts to pass the tool along the work several times to ensure that the hole is the full depth right through its length. Cutting fluids should be used where appropriate.

these implements can either be made from solid steel or can have an interchangeable tip. They are known as boring bars and many people find it preferable to make their own rather than try to buy one of a suitable size. They are quite easy to make, consisting of little more than a length of steel, cross-drilled to accept a tiny piece of high-speed steel ground to the shape of a cutting tool. They can also be bought or made with carbide and similar tips.

Boring Between Centres

A far more accurate way of boring holes is to mount the work on the saddle and use a boring bar swung between centres – as a result, there is no flexing of the tool because it is supported at each end. In general this method is only suitable for quite large holes and of course cannot be used with a blind bore. It is particularly useful where the shape of a casting makes it impossible to mount it on the mandrel.

Knurling

Knurling is the name given to a process that applies an indented pattern on to the work, and it is usually used on applications where some sort of grip on the metal will be required, such as hand tools. Knurling involves forcing into the work specially made hardened wheels, which have a suitable pattern impregnated in such a way that cutting edges are formed on the pattern. There are several types of knurling tools. Some consist of little more than a bar of metal with the wheel in the end, which is simply pushed into the work while it is rotating and the sheer force creates the pattern. If a

diamond pattern is intended the device will probably consist of two wheels, but the principle of operation remains exactly the same. In general, in the home workshop where machinery tends to be of much lighter construction than in industry it is not the best type of tool to use, as a lot of pressure is put on the headstock bearings and can create wear.

Other types of knurling tools have adjustable calipers holding the wheels, with the result that most of the pressure is taken on the adjuster rather than on the lathe bearings. These are far more suitable when used on a lightly constructed lathe.

A Caliper pattern knurling tool, consisting of a plate either side of the two arms, which are tightened by the screw in the centre. Making it is an ideal project for the workshop.

Knurling Wheels

Various types of knurling wheels are available, and if the pattern is to be diamond-shaped it is usual to use two diagonal wheels, the diagonal pattern on each one going at opposite angles. Once the wheels have been engaged with the work and have gone to the full depth, they may

A Caliper knurling tool that fits in the tailstock, thus preventing any side thrust on the lathe bearings. This, too, is a home-made product and as far as is known is not commercially available.

An end-on view of the tailstock-held Caliper showing how the wheels are adjusted to fit on the work.

be moved along to obtain the required pattern length. Slow speeds should always be used, and in addition a cutting fluid must be applied as a great deal of heat is generated by the knurling process.

Filing

Finishing work with a file while it is rotating is not something to be generally recommended, although there are occasions when it might be necessary to use a file to blend in contours. In such instances, a filing rest should be used to support the file and care must be taken to ensure that injury is not caused by the rotating mandrel. The actual finish of a piece of work will never be enhanced by finishing with a file or other abrasive material, all of which result in undesirable scratches on the work. Nothing betters a good fine finishing cut, traversed slowly along the length of the work. There may

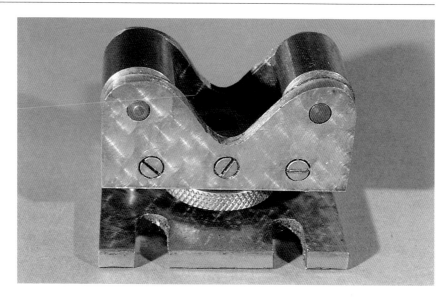

A filing rest, the rollers ensure that the file stays level and prevent it from slipping.

at times be a need to use a file to obtain a flat surface on a piece of work, and this too should be done using a filing rest and with the mandrel locked in a static position to prevent unwanted movement. A roller filing rest is used, although it is doubtful if it will be possible to buy such a tool. A rest is not difficult to make and is well worth the little time involved in so doing.

SCREW CUTTING

Threads up to about the diameter of 6mm (0.25in) can generally be made by using a die, held in a special holder in the lathe tailstock.

Anything larger needs to be cut by using the lathe facilities, assuming of course the lathe is so fitted. By changing the relationship of the saddle movement when using the safe-act facility to the rotation of the mandrel, the saddle can be made to travel at a given distance per rotation, which is designed to match the pitch of the required thread. This adjustment is made either by changing gear wheels at the end of the mandrel, or by using a gearbox, if the lathe has one. It will be necessary to fit a thread dial indicator, if the lathe does not already have one. The TDI, as it is generally referred to, indicates at what position the lead screw is

A tailstock die holder, made in two sections. The die fits the non-tapered section, which can slide along the other part as the cutting of the thread progresses.

locked on to the nut on the saddle to make it move.

It will be seen from the thread charts in the appendix that different types of threads have different angles, and so a tool needs to be ground to match exactly the required one. A special gauge is used to check this. The work to be threaded is machined to size, and the top slide turned to an angle of exactly half that of the thread and the tool set exactly square, using the same gauge that was used to check the thread angles. When the lathe is started, the TDI starts to rotate and the lead screw should be engaged with the TDI at one of the large figures, each time it is re-engaged it should be at the same figure, which will then ensure the saddle movement will commence at exactly the same point each time. Some fine threads allow for the nut to be engaged at half or even a quarter of the original position, but unless certain whether that will work, stick to using the same figure each time.

The depth of the cut is increased at each cut by advancing the top slide, which not only makes the groove deeper but also wider. The finished depth will depend on two factors, whether it is to remain as cut or, as is preferable, finished with a die. If a suitable die is not available, finish the thread with wire wool and oil to give it a clean finish. When cutting threads, there should always be an undercut at the end at which the tool is to be released, to allow it to be clear of any metal. If there is no undercut, it becomes very difficult to judge at which point the tool should be lifted and damage can result. An undercut is always desirable at the end of a thread, even when it is made with a die, as otherwise it is not possible to screw the thread completely home into its mating component.

Internal Threads

Small internal threads should be made with taps. Generally they can be held either in the tailstock chuck, or better still in a special tap holder designed for the job. If for any reason it is not practical to use the tailstock chuck, a tap wrench supported by the tailstock mandrel will assist in keeping the thread square. Larger threads can be screw cut in a similar manner to that described for external ones, and here the necessity for an undercut is even more important if threading a blind hole. The big problem when cutting an internal thread is judging the depth – the only way to see how good the thread is will be to use a threaded component as a test piece.

TAPER TURNING

Short Tapers

Short tapers can be made by using the top slide, either using the graduations or by setting up using a known taper. This perhaps needs some explanation – set up the known taper either between centres, or if necessary use a chuck, then put a flat bar of metal in the tool post and check that it runs parallel to the lathe bed. Without moving the bar in the tool post, turn the top slide over until the bar is exactly parallel with the known taper; use either feeler gauges or a spacer to check that it is right. Tighten the top slide, which should now be at the required angle, checking with a clock gauge to make certain.

A gauge giving thread angles. It is used as a guide for grinding tools with which to cut the thread and then laid against the face of the chuck or the work and used as a guide to ensure that the tool is set square.

Above *Using a tap in the tailstock chuck to tap a component. Only large diameter taps should be used in this way; small diameters should be mounted in a holder that allows them to slide.*

Right *Checking the set over of a top slide with a clock gauge.*

Long Tapers

Longer tapers are always machined between centres, using either a special taper-turning attachment that automatically draws the cross slide to the required position as it travels, or, if it is possible to do so, moving the tailstock over. The latter operation may not be possible on many lathes, and it can in any case create problems when it comes to setting it back accurately. A way round this is to make a special device, consisting of a bar of metal, held in the tailstock, with an offset centre at the required distance from the original centre.

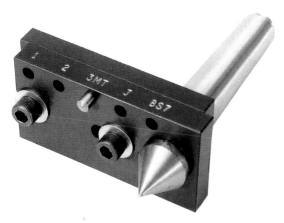

A commercially made device for offsetting work in order to machine a taper. There are settings for a number of different tapers.

PARTING OFF

Parting off is possibly the most unpopular of all operations carried out on a lathe and that is no doubt the reason why some people would rather saw and face the work. Unless used properly, parting tools have a nasty habit of digging into the work and snapping, and it is this that makes the operation so unpopular. However, with a little thought and care there is no need whatever why the tool should snap.

The Reasons Why

Broken parting tools are almost invariably the result of a lack of rigidity of one type or another. It may be that the tool is not held securely in either its holder or the tool post, or that the bearings of the lathe have sufficient give in them to allow the tool to dig into the work. To carry out parting off successfully, the tool needs to be held rigidly, the saddle and cross slide as well as the tool post need to be well adjusted, and the tool must be sharp and at centre height. In addition, the rotational speed as well as the speed that the tool is taken into the work need to be right, and if necessary, the correct cutting fluid should be used. Plenty of people carry out the operation every day and no difficulties occur, but it only needs one of the above factors to be wrong for disaster to strike.

A Rear Tool Post

An easy solution is to use a rear tool post. This works from the opposite side of the lathe bed to the normal one, with the result that any movement of the mandrel is forced against the lathe bed and cannot move, so the most common reason for broken tools is no longer present. This is not a reason for not trying to get all the other necessary factors right as they are still important, but the extra rigidity does make up for any unavoidable difficulties.

Making a Rear Tool Post

It is not always easy or desirable to buy a rear tool post and for many imported lathes they simply are not available, but they are so easy to make that it is hardly worth the bother of buying one. Take a suitable length of square mild steel or cast iron and use a four-jaw chuck to face both ends where the metal has been cut; at the same time drill a hole through the centre, to accept a tee bolt. Bolt it firmly to the cross slide and with a milling cutter in the lathe chuck or collet, make a slot in which the parting tool can be located. Take the work off the lathe, and drill and tap three or four holes that can be used for bolting the tool into the post. There you have it – a tool post that can be mounted on the rear of the cross slide, except that it may not yet be quite right for doing the job, as many cross slides are too short to allow a

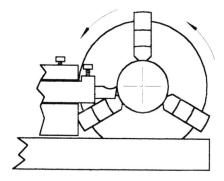

Usual position for turning tool

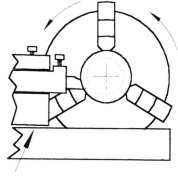

If a parting tool is used in the normal position, excessive speed of tool travel can cause it to dig into the work, in turn this will lift and push the mandrel sideways making the tool dig in deeper still and eventually causing it to snap.

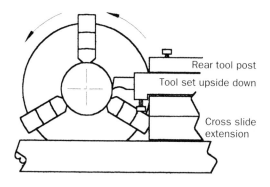

Rear tool post
Tool set upside down

Cross slide extension

Reverse position for parting tool

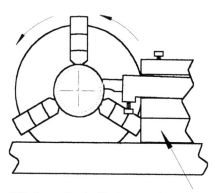

With the parting tool in the rear should the tool dig too deep the rotation of the lathe will now force it away from the work making it less likely to break.

Diagrams showing reasons for parting-off operations to be carried out from the rear of the machine.

rear tool post to be fitted unless the top slide is removed, which is an unsatisfactory situation.

A length of plate can be used to cure the problem. It needs to have two holes to allow it to be bolted firmly to the cross slide and a stud for holding the tool post. Do ensure that it has sufficient support though, by giving it an overlap of at least 35mm (1.5in), otherwise there is the danger of damaging the cross slide, not to mention the work. The bar used

to make the rear tool post will need to be reduced in length to allow for the additional height of this extension. It will be found that with this set-up that parting off problems become be a thing of the past. However, it must be remembered that the rotation of the lathe from the new angle means that the cutting edge of the tool will have to be in the opposite position to normal, or, in other words, upside down.

145

A rear tool post and extension fitted with a parting tool.

This chunky tool post is ideal for use at the rear. The three slotted screws are made with the heads off-centre and by rotating them the height of the tool can be adjusted.

OTHER OPERATIONS

There are numerous other operations that can be carried out on a lathe. With the use of a vertical slide it can be used for milling; a special adaptor will allow slotting operations; it can cut gear wheels; and be used for fly-cutting. In fact, almost the only limitations to what it will do are governed by its size and the imagination of the operator. It is indeed a machine that should be looked after, as it will then last a lifetime and handsomely repay whatever it may have cost.

9 Milling

Milling can briefly be described as the opposite of turning. Whereas in the latter operation the work is revolved against a specially prepared cutting tool, when milling the tool itself is rotated and brought into contact with the work. The result of this is the generation of a flat plane, instead of a curved one. Although these days milling machines are commonplace in small workshops, this has not always been the case and the humble lathe was invariably used for both purposes. It is intended in this chapter to deal mainly with the use of a milling machine, but there are still many people who do not possess such a tool and adapt their lathe in one way or another for the purpose. This may be because the cost of a milling machine is not thought to be justifiable when the type of work being carried out is considered or it could just be lack of space in the workshop. Traditionally when milling in a lathe a device called a vertical slide has been used, consisting of a slotted platform on which to secure work that has a rise and fall mechanism and is mounted on the cross slide. A more modern method is to use a specially made milling head, bolted to the lathe, in which the milling cutter can be mounted, which is powered either by the lathe mandrel or a separate motor. The cross slide of the lathe is then used as the milling table. It is even possible to purchase machines that are made with such a device permanently built in place, which are specially designed to be used where space is limited.

HORIZONTAL MILLING MACHINES

Machines made specially for milling can in general be divided into two types, horizontal and vertical. In the former the cutter rotates, as the name would suggest, on a horizontal plane and the cutters look like saw blades, although they are often quite wide are mounted on an arbor. They traverse the work, which is mounted on the table, and are ideal for removing large areas of metal. Because of the diameter of the cutters the machines are usually designed to rotate at fairly slow speeds. Different thicknesses of cutters can be used for cutting keyways and similar operations. Small machines can generally be bought on the second-hand market, considerably more cheaply than the vertical type because the high cost of cutters can mean that without considerable expenditure their use may be limited. On the plus side, they are generally much more rigid than the vertical milling machine and so give a far better finish to work.

VERTICAL MILLING MACHINES

By far the most popular type of milling machine, using the same principle as the milling device built on to a lathe or a vertical slide, the vertical milling machine is generally speaking more adaptable than the horizontal one. Unlike the horizontal machine, where the cutters are mounted on an arbor, a special

A small vertical milling machine which is ideal for a small workshop.

chuck is held in the mandrel of the machine, and milling cutters fit directly into this. The fact that the cutter is only supported at one end does make it liable to chatter and any lack of rigidity in work-holding can result in an uneven cut. Some vertical milling machines have a swivelling head, allowing the cutter to be used at an angle, a system that can occasionally be of use when angled cutting is required.

Universal

It is possible to obtain milling machines designed for both horizontal and vertical milling. These are the true universal machines, giving one the best of both worlds. They generally will only be available on the used market.

Work-Holding

Whatever machining operations are carried out on any type of machine, secure work-holding is absolutely essential and there are basically two ways of doing this on a milling machine.

BOLTING TO THE TABLE

The work can be bolted directly to the table, in which case a minimum of three clamping positions should be aimed for. The end of the clamp away from the work must always be supported higher than the end that is to be used for securing, in order to bring sufficient pressure to bear on the work. It may be necessary to support work in such a way that it is clear of the milling table, in order to prevent damage to the table by the milling cutter. A stock of suitable bars of flat material or sections of round bar should be kept for this purpose, and these are generally referred to as parallels. In industry, these would be ground to a specific size and ground parallels can be purchased if one wishes. The problem that arises is the fact that one never knows quite what thickness is likely to be needed and invariably it is likely to be inconvenient to have to purchase suitable parallels when in the middle of setting up a job. For most purposes, therefore, ordinary mild

An aluminium casting bolted directly to the table of a vertical milling machine while fly-cutting operations are carried out.

steel bar will do, providing that the size is checked for accuracy, alternatively part off lengths of a round bar or use washers.

Sometimes odd shapes, such as castings, need machining and bolting these accurately to the table is difficult. It is usual to use small screw jacks to give support where required. These are invariably home-made to whatever size is thought most suitable; they are frequently made in several parts so that they can be extended if required. If very thin material is to be milled it can be impossible to clamp it to the table because the clamps would get in the way of operations. A way to hold it is to get a piece of steel plate, about 10–12mm thick, and use it as a sub-table. Clamp the plate to the table and stick the work to it with double-sided adhesive tape, making sure before using it that both the plate and the work have been thoroughly degreased.

The Milling Vice

Work can be held securely in a properly designed milling vice bolted firmly to the table. Care must be taken to ensure that the jaws are square to the line of the cut. This can be done using a clock gauge. The final tightening down

Home-made screw jacks like these can be used to adjust awkwardly shaped castings that are being bolted to the milling table.

of the milling vice frequently results in a tiny movement that destroys the careful setting. A trick used by old-time craftsmen to prevent this from happening was to lay a sheet of paper, preferably a fairly absorbent piece, between the vice and the table. This absorbed the shock created by the rotary action of the spanner used

for tightening and ensured that the vice stayed in place. Many milling vices suffer from the problem that when tightened the moving jaw tends to tilt, leaving the work at an angle. This is usually hardly visible to the naked eye, but is sufficient to cause an error, particularly in the case of work requiring high precision. There are two ways to cure the problem. The first is to set the work in the jaws together with a length of round bar between it and the moving jaw, and as the jaws are tightened to give the work a

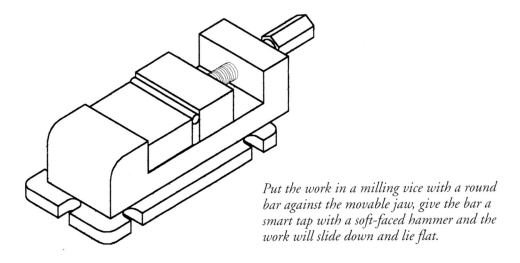

Put the work in a milling vice with a round bar against the movable jaw, give the bar a smart tap with a soft-faced hammer and the work will slide down and lie flat.

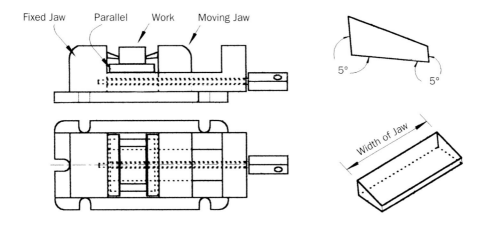

The drawing gives details of how to make small wedges that will force work in the vice down flat.

smart tap with a soft hammer. It will then slide down the round bar and settle on the base, remaining flat. The second method is to make some wedges and insert these; they will automatically pull the work down. However, this method may result in some loss of strength of the grip obtained by the vice and is best reserved for lighter work.

CUTTERS

Cutters for Horizontal Machines

Horizontal milling machines use a range of cutters that vary in diameter and thickness as well as in the pitch of the teeth. In addition, some are shaped in order to produce various radii, internal or external. They are mounted on the arbor with packing pieces, and these pieces are also available in the form of shims that enable several cutters to be mounted at specific intervals, thus allowing two or more slots at predetermined intervals to be cut at the same time. Cutting speeds are generally in direct relationship to the diameter of the cutter and the material being machined. In all cases where it is steel that is being dealt with, a continuous flow of coolant is required.

Cutters for Vertical Machines

There are several types of cutter used on vertical machines. Those with four flutes are called end mills and where they only have two flutes they are described as slot drills. As the names imply, the latter are or were originally devised for cutting slots, although they now find general use in all sorts of operations. Nevertheless, if they are to be used for milling slots, the task for which they are most suitable, it should be borne in mind that if extreme accuracy is required the direction of travel should be in one direction only. The cutter should then be lifted and returned to its original position, before again being lowered to take the next cut. Taking a cut in the reverse direction will inevitably result in the slot being cut oversize. A more recent innovation has been the introduction of three-flute cutters that are intended to do a combined job of end milling and slot cutting. They do generally cope quite well with both tasks, whereas the end mill is not efficient when it comes to cutting slots and a slot drill gives a less than satisfactory finish if the sides are used. In addition to the plain cutters referred to above, a variety of specially shaped cutters can be obtained for making dovetails and slots, such as tee slots.

A three-flute cutter in use.

Using the side of a three-flute cutter.

Using a dovetail cutter.

A small slot cutter in use, cutting ports in a cylinder casting.

Milling cutters are held in the machine with collets that are fitted in special adaptors that have tapers for accurate location. The type of adaptor required varies according to the particular machine. At one time, all small milling machines had Morse Tapers, but more modern machines now have a different system employing a shorter and stubbier taper. One thing all holders have in common is the fact that they are positively held in the machine with a draw bar. The way the cutter is prevented from rotating varies according to the holder. Some accept cutters with threaded ends and others locate with cutters that have a short flat surface on them. In general, only the cutter designed for a particular type of holder should

These are Morse taper split collets that can be used with some machines without the use of a collet holder. Positive location and security are provided with a draw bar.

be used as other types will not lock positively. This can result in the cutter slowly winding in or out during operations, resulting in it being impossible to obtain a true depth of cut and damage to the work can occur where the cutter has worked its way out.

OPERATING THE MILLING MACHINE

As with all machines, it is essential that the milling cutter rotates at a more or less correct speed for the metal being worked on and in relation to the diameter of the cutter. A good flow of cutting fluid is essential when working on steel in order to prevent the cutter from overheating. The cutter should not be fed too deep into the work, and the work should be traversed at a speed that will avoid any overheating taking place. A milling cutter generates more heat than we get from turning operations on the lathe and it is something that must be considered. When using slotting or dovetail cutters, care needs to be taken as the cutter breaks out from the end of the operation as this is the time when there is the greatest strain, and cutters, particularly those for dovetails, are likely to break.

Cutters should always be used so that the teeth drive into the work. This is known as up-cut milling; working in the opposite direction is called climb milling, and as the name suggests there is a tendency for the cutter to climb over the work, which results not only in a bad finish but also a loss of accuracy. It is essential that cutters are kept sharp, but to do so requires special equipment. Many people make their own cutter grinders and variety of designs for these are available. The alternative is to take them to a specialist to be sharpened. This is not an expensive process and many good tool shops have sharpening capabilities.

Fly-Cutting
A fly-cutter is a single-point tool, more often than not home-made, and is used on large flat surfaces. Strangely enough, a fly-cutter will usually give a better finish to work than that obtained by using a more conventional cutter. For best results, the sweep of the cutter should be sufficient to cover the whole width of the job and should always be operated at a slow speed.

Boring
Many vertical milling machines are now made to act as both milling and drilling machines, and as such it is quite possible to fit a drill chuck and use a normal twist drill. There are times though when larger holes or recesses are needed and these are machined with a device

A facing and boring head with micrometer adjustment for accurate boring of holes.

known as a facing and boring head, which is very similar to the fly-cutter. Indeed, there is no reason why a fly-cutter should not be used for such operations, except that it is very difficult to adjust. The difference with a facing and boring head is that it has a micrometer-type adjustment that allows it to be used to a high degree of accuracy. Once again, is a tool that is comparatively easy to make for oneself.

Circular Work

Work requiring the generation of curved surfaces is done with the aid of a rotary table. It is a device consisting of a table with slots to which work can be bolted that is laid on to a base. The rotation of a handle in the base in turn rotates the table and micrometer readings on a dial give an indication of the degree of rotation that has occurred. Rotary tables

A boring head in use on a casting.

generally can be used in horizontal or vertical positions and are available in a wide range of sizes.

Setting Up

In order to use a milling machine properly it is of course essential that the work is correctly set and that the cutter is used accurately both as regards depth of cut and position on the work. It is not advisable to work to lines that are scribed on the job as these quickly become difficult to see, marking fluid washes off when in contact with cutting mediums, and no matter how sharp the cutter there is always the possibility of the build-up of a burr to conceal the line. The answer is to use the graduations of the machine, not forgetting to allow for backlash, which is always going to be present to a lesser or greater degree. A way of avoiding the backlash problem is to fit a digital read-out of one sort or another. These can be purchased or a cheap alternative can be devised by using a vernier-type calliper with a digital read-out. Simply make a couple of brackets, one to secure the jaws to the table and the other to fit the body to the base of the machine. As the table

A rotary table is used to generate curved surfaces and tables are available in a wide variety of sizes. The one shown is another product of the home workshop.

moves, so will the calliper jaw and the amount of movement can be read on the scale. It is true that the distance of travel that can be read by this set-up is not large, but in general this sort of accuracy is only needed over short lengths.

Finding Where to Start

No matter how accurately the distance of travel can be read, it is of absolutely no use unless one knows where the cutter is to start with, and the tool used for this is known as an edge finder. It is a metal tube that accepts a round ball held in place with a spring and cap. There is a spigot on the ball that goes either to another ball, a cylinder or a point. The tube is located in the mandrel of the milling machine and let us say the ball on the end of the spigot is brought in contact with the work. The machine is rotated and when the spigot is seen to be running true, the centre of the mandrel is exactly half the distance of the ball away from the edge. Simply

A simple digital read-out made by fixing a cheap digital depth gauge, bought on a market stall, to the milling machine.

move the table by half the diameter and the mandrel is known to be exactly central to the edge of the work. It all sounds very complicated but is really the simplest possible idea and by using it the position of the centre of the milling machine mandrel can be accurately located.

Knowing exactly when a cutter as it is lowered is likely to come into contact with the work is best achieved by a most primitive system. Take a short piece of cigarette paper and coat it in oil, then lay it flat on the surface to be machined. Bring the cutter down gently and as soon as it snatches the paper it will be 0.007mm ($\frac{2}{1000}$ in) above the work. The same system can be used to locate the side of the work instead of using the edge finder.

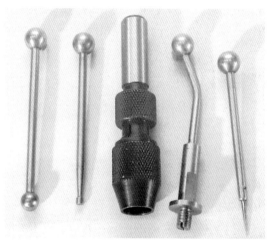

The parts of an edge finder. The large ball fits in the body and the other pieces are used to locate accurately the mandrel centre. The arm on the immediate right of the body is designed to accept a clock gauge.

10 Tool Sharpening

It is essential that a keen edge be maintained on all cutting tools. If they are allowed to blunt it will be impossible to obtain a good finish, metal will be heavily scored and large burrs raised. This applies to all types of work, from marking out to milling. There are two things that are essential to good tool sharpening – a grinding wheel and a honing device of some sort. The latter is essential because like any

A standard type of bench grinder with a coarse and fine wheel.

other machining operation when a tool is ground burrs build up on the edges and these need to be removed, otherwise they will spoil the performance of the tool.

GRINDERS

A grinding machine, or off-hand grinder as they are known, will generally take the form of a bench-mounted device consisting of an electric motor with a grinding wheel on each side, each of which are of a differing texture.

The size of the machine will depend on the diameter of wheel that it is designed to accept and the size chosen for the home workshop will depend on what space is available. The largest size that can be accommodated should be chosen, for reasons that we will come to later. Like many things in the home workshop, there may have to be a compromise and sometimes people with limited space will choose a machine that is fitted with a wheel at one end and a spindle at the other, on which some other device, possibly a polishing wheel, can be fitted. There is nothing wrong in doing this, as a polishing wheel can be an extremely useful item and may even be essential to the type of work being undertaken, but it does mean that the grinding wheel will need to be something of a compromise.

Before thinking of any other form of abrasive, let us first of all explore the off-hand grinder in detail. It is one of the most important machines in the workshop and properly used will be an invaluable aid to good workmanship. It can also be one of the most dangerous machines if treated carelessly, and yet in spite of that it is all too often greatly abused. The grinder consists of nothing more than an electric motor with a spindle protruding from each end on which the wheels are mounted. It is frequently controlled by a switch that allows only a single speed; better quality machines will have a range of speeds. Most of the wheel area should be surrounded by a shield and it must be fitted with a shield over the top of the part of the wheel that is left uncovered. A platform should be fitted at each

wheel on which to support the tool that is being ground. Both the guards and support platforms need to be adjustable and it should be possible to replace the shield easily as these soon become opaque.

GRINDING WHEELS

Every machine is made to accept wheels of a certain size, and no other size should be used. On this type of machine the wheels are plain discs and more often than not this is the only type of grinding wheel that will concern the home metalworker. A few people will invest in special grinding machines for sharpening milling cutters, in which case the wheel will be cup-shaped, but it is not proposed to deal with these here as they are very specialized. All grinding wheels are manufactured in the same way – tiny particles of abrasive material are bonded together to form the required shape, and particles of grit of differing sizes will determine how quickly the wheel will remove metal and the appearance of the finished result. The size of the grit, or grain as it is sometimes referred to, is produced to an international

The label on the wheel is very important, as it supplies essential information and helps to prevent the wheel from breaking up.

Worn Bearings

Apart from the wheels, the only parts that can wear are the bearings at each end of the motor and these should be checked for play from time to time. If there is more than 3mm side play accuracy can be lost. It should be possible to fit thrust washers to take up the slack if movement is found.

standard, at least as far as Europe is concerned, the standard being set by the Federation of European Producers of Abrasive Products. Some wheel manufacture in other parts of the world may vary, but the majority will be to the European Standard. The size of the grit will be denoted on the wheel and the larger the number, the smaller the grit. For example, a grain sized ten will be 2mm, while grit of 0.25mm is grain size sixty. Although most people will buy a wheel as coarse, medium or fine, it is worth knowing the grain size in order to get one suited to one's own requirements. For example, a wheel suitable for sharpening large drills will not be suitable if very tiny drills are being sharpened, when a much finer grain size is required.

BONDING MATERIALS

There are a number of materials used for bonding and these too have a bearing on what the wheel should be used for. As a tool is sharpened the grit is worn away, together with some of the bonding, with the result that fresh grit is continually exposed – if this did not happen, in no time at all the wheel would have no effect. To some extent the bonding material controls how quickly this is done, therefore the bonding is as important to the end result as the grit. Although there is a whole variety of bonding materials, it is only necessary to concern oneself with those that will suit the operations likely to be found in the home workshop.

Vitrified bond refers to a wheel where the abrasive material is bonded with a vitreous material such as glass, and as such wheels are cured at temperatures exceeding 1,000°C they will withstand high temperatures when in use. For example, where a considerable amount of metal has to be removed, a lot of heat is generated. Organic bonds are usually rubber and shellac and are cured at a much lower temperature than the vitrified bond; therefore they wear much more quickly, particularly if too much heat is generated when they are used.

Resinoid bonds are made mainly from synthetic resins; sometimes a filler is added, with the result that the wheel is more flexible and can withstand considerable heat. These wheels tend to give a finer finish than wheels with an identical grit but a different bonding material.

GRITS

A variety of substances can be ground down to form the grit of the wheel, but in the main the average enthusiast will only use aluminium oxide, which has a characteristic brown colour. White aluminium oxide is generally used for cup wheels. Silicon carbide is used on particularly hard materials and is necessary to sharpen tools made of tungsten carbide. These are generally called green grit wheels, because of their colour, which although always green can vary in shade. The lighter coloured wheel is most suitable if it is to be used with tungsten carbide. Because the material to be ground is so tough, the bond is designed to wear away rather more quickly than normal, thus bringing a constant supply of new grit to the surface to do the work.

FITTING WHEELS TO MACHINES

Wheels are mounted on the mandrel of the grinding machine and the securing thread on the left-hand side will be left-handed so that it will not come undone when used. Because of the variation in diameters of shafts, manufacturers of the wheels supply plastic bushes to enable the wheels to be adapted to a particular diameter. On all wheels there is a or should be a label, which not only gives the specification of the wheel but also helps to ensure that the wheel does not crack or break around the securing point. This label under no circumstances should be removed and a large cup washer must be fitted each side of the hole. Before fitting the wheel it is advisable to check that it is sound, and apart from looking for obvious signs of damage a

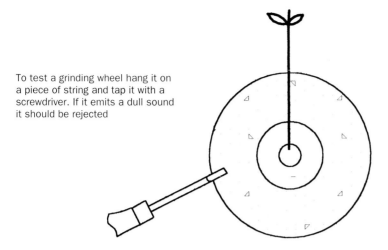

To test a grinding wheel hang it on a piece of string and tap it with a screwdriver. If it emits a dull sound it should be rejected

A drawing showing the method of testing to see whether a grinding wheel is sound.

ringing test should be carried out. It is not complicated – simply support the wheel on a length of string, ensuring that it is not touching any other object, and gently tap it in a few places around the periphery with a screwdriver. If the wheel is sound it will emit a ringing tone; if not, there will be a dull flat sound and the wheel should be discarded. It is, of course, necessary to ensure that the nuts holding the wheel to the spindle are tight. Do not, however, over-tighten, in case the pressure applied causes the wheel to crack.

Dangerous Wheels

A cracked or broken grinding wheel is a thing of great danger, as it is capable of literally exploding into a thousand pieces while rotating at full speed and can do great damage. The force created is incredible and exploding wheels have been known to badly damage machinery as well as causing serious injuries. More often than not, a factory would have one or two people specially trained in dealing with grinders and they and they alone would be allowed to change wheels. This cannot be applied of course to a home workshop, but great care must be taken with anything related to the grindstone.

GRINDSTONE LABELS

The label attached to a new grindstone is very important as it displays all the facts one needs to know about the stone, although it is necessary to know what the figures mean to get at some of that information. The most important thing that is written on there as far as the amateur is concerned is the maximum rotational speed at which the stone can be used. It is unlikely that a grinding machine of the type generally found in the home workshop would have a speed greater than the maximum permitted speed of the wheel, but amateurs do obtain some of their equipment in unusual ways and it might just happen that a stone which outwardly appears to be alright is in fact made for some purpose that restricts its working speed to lower than that of the machine.

USING THE GRINDSTONE

The machine must never be used without eye protection and wearing gloves is also advisable. Apart from the danger of the work slipping and causing an injury to the hands, it can also get very hot and cause nasty burns if held in the

161

bare hands. Some people like to have a small container of water or other cooling medium by the grindstone in which to cool the water off, but this can do more harm than good. If the metal gets too hot and is immediately quenched it could harden and become too brittle, causing it to break when in use. A grindstone should never be used for anything other than sharpening tools. If soft metal is used it clogs the wheel and reduces its efficiency. Removing large amounts of softer metal should be done with an abrasive band machine or some other rotational grinding device.

In theory, only the periphery of the wheel should be used because this ensures that any force is applied to the strongest point. If the side is used, the strength is only equal to the wheel thickness, whereas at the periphery it equals the diameter. There is no doubt that theoretically this is correct, but it is not entirely practical and without doubt wrong though it may be, a large part of grinding is carried out on the side of the wheel. Like many things in life, therefore, although not the thing to do it is a standard practice, and the only advice that can be offered for such a practice is to use the lightest possible pressure and to ensure that any work carried out on the side of the wheel is not always done in the same place, but that the whole area is used.

Grinding Jigs

Details of the correct cutting angles for tools have been given in the relevant chapters. It takes many years to develop the skill to be able simply to sharpen a tool by hand and get the angle right, and so it is usual to use grinding jigs or some other aid. There is a whole range of jigs for sharpening drills on the market and at remarkably cheap prices; all appear to be quite capable of doing the job for which they are designed. It is also possible to purchase special attachments that fit on hand-held DIY-type electric drills. For anyone not having room for a grinder these are worth considering; some also catch the dust created by the grinding, which is a very good thing.

Grinding Dust

The dust imparted by grinding tools can be the curse of a small workshop. This dust consists of a mixture of bond and abrasive. If it gets into the bearings or slide ways on any machine it will rapidly cause wear, and so every possible precaution must be taken to ensure that this does not happen. If we are not careful that dust will also be inhaled and one shudders to think of the damage it might do, so take care to ensure that it is not breathed in: always wear a mask.

LATHE TOOLS

Some people like to make jigs that allow them to get the correct cutting angles on lathe tools. It is not really necessary to do so, however, as the tool rest is designed exactly for that purpose, and can be set to the required angle with a protractor. It is with the sharpening of lathe tools in a workshop that has only this type of grinder that we see one of the problems of only using the periphery of the wheel, because instead of getting a straight edge it will have an internal radius. It will cause a slight weakening of the tool, but otherwise will not matter too much, and is another reason to buy a machine with wheels as large as possible, because the larger the wheel the shallower the radius.

Milling Cutters

Strictly speaking, sharpening milling cutters on an off-hand grinder is not terribly practical – they should be sharpened on a properly designed machine. For most people this will mean taking them to a tool supplier to be sent away for sharpening. Certainly it is not advisable to sharpen cutters for horizontal machines, but it is possible to make a reasonable job of the end cutting edges, which are the edges mostly used. It requires a simple jig, which is easily made and usually the support table on the grinder will need to be enlarged and possibly strengthened a little as well. The jig shown in the drawing has a fine

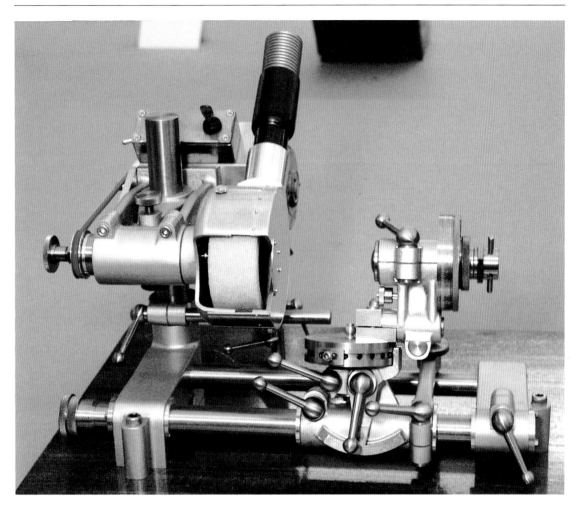

Above *A special machine for sharpening milling cutters, lathe tools and so on.*

Right *A jig that enables the cutting edges of slot drills and end mills to be sharpened. It should be set at the correct cutting angle on the grinding machine table and clamped in position.*

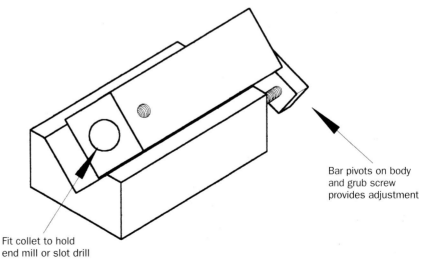

Fit collet to hold end mill or slot drill

Bar pivots on body and grub screw provides adjustment

adjusting screw that allows all edges to be cut to the same depth.

Centre Punches
To regrind the point on a centre punch set the table on the grinder to whatever angle will suit the tool, bring the point to the stone and rotate the tool. Use only the very lightest of pressure and do not allow it to overheat.

Scribers
A scriber should never be sharpened on a grinding wheel. It should be rubbed lengthways on a piece of emery cloth laid on a flat surface and rotated at the same time.

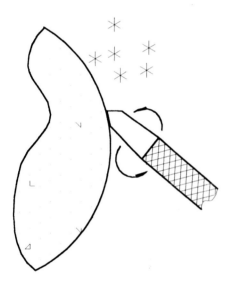

A centre punch should be rotated as it is sharpened.

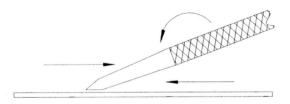

Never sharpen a scriber on a grinding wheel. Use a piece of abrasive paper laid flat and rub the point up and down while rotating it at the same time.

Taps
If a tap becomes blunt it will quickly ruin any work it is being used on. Like milling cutters, taps should be dealt with on a special machine, but again it is possible to improve their cutting qualities. It requires the use of one of the tiny cylindrical grinding stones that are available in model and craft shops, which can be run along the flutes at the cutting edge. Most taps have a

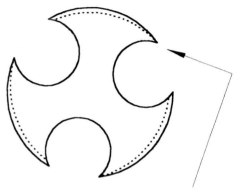

To sharpen tap inset small cylindrical stone in clearance groove and grind cutting edge

It is possible to sharpen a tap by running a small cylindrical grinding wheel in the clearance groove.

To sharpen the die run small cylindrical stone against cutting edge

A die can also be sharpened by using a small cylindrical grinding wheel in the clearance holes.

concentric thread without relief behind the cutting face and will stand several sharpenings in this fashion. With very small taps it is possible to use a tiny disc to do the same job, and these are also available at toy and craft shops. Take care as the discs break very easily if too much pressure is applied.

Dies

A die can also damage work if it is not sharp. In order to maintain a reasonable edge it is possible to adopt the same idea as used for a tap – a tiny cylindrical stone can be run in the clearance holes against the cutting edge and this will be sufficient to keep the die sharp.

HONING

Oilstones

Wherever possible, a tool should be honed after grinding, as doing so ensures a much superior finish to the work and small oilstones are available in a wide variety of shapes and sizes. Two abrasives are used in their manufacture, aluminium oxide and silicon carbide, each in a variety of grades. For most purposes, a medium grade will be sufficient.

Whetstones

The term whetstone has traditionally been applied to large, slow rotating grindstones used by the woodworker for the sharpening of plane irons and chisels, but now it has come to mean a diamond-impregnated stone, which for larger work is rapidly superseding the oilstone. Small ones can be obtained that are particularly suitable for honing lathe tools and many are designed to be folded and put away in a pocket. They are extremely good for honing lathe tools, but because they are generally much larger than the oilstone they are not suitable for very small work.

Appendix I
Thread Sizes

SHEET METAL SIZES AND WIRE SIZES

Sheet metal and wire are sold according to their thickness. Sheet is now always in metric. Most older plans will specify either imperial or SWG sizes. The table should offer help in deciding the thickness required. Only common sizes are shown. There are forty two sizes. Wire is still commonly sold by gauge.

Metric	Decimal	SWG	Decimal
6mm	0.2362	4	0.2320
5mm	0.1969	6	0.1920
4mm	0.1575	8	0.1600
3mm	0.1181	10	0.1280
2.5mm	0.0984	12	0.1040
2.0mm	0.0787	13	0.0920
1.0mm	0.0384	16	0.0640
0.9mm	0.0354	18	0.0480
0.8mm	0.0315	20	0.0360
0.7mm	0.0276	22	0.0280
0.6mm	0.0236	24	0.0220
0.5mm	0.0200	26	0.0180
		28	0.0148
		30	0.0124

BRITISH STANDARD WHITWORTH (BSW)

Size	Threads Per Inch	Tapping Drill	Clearance Drill
$\frac{1}{16}$ in	60	1.4	1.7
$\frac{3}{32}$ in	48	2.1	2.5
$\frac{1}{8}$ in	40	2.6	3.3
$\frac{3}{16}$ in	24	3.9	4.8
$\frac{1}{4}$ in	20	5.10	6.40
$\frac{5}{16}$ in	18	6.50	8.00
$\frac{3}{8}$ in	16	7.90	9.60
$\frac{7}{16}$ in	14	9.30	11.20
$\frac{1}{2}$ in	12	10.50	12.70
$\frac{9}{16}$ in	12	12.10	14.50
$\frac{5}{8}$ in	11	13.50	16.00
$\frac{11}{16}$ in	11	15.00	17.50
$\frac{3}{4}$ in	10	16.25	19.25
$\frac{7}{8}$ in	9	19.25	22.25
1in	8	22.00	25.50

UNIFIED FINE THREADS (UNF), (ANF) OR (A/F)

Size Numbers	TPI	Tapping Drill	Clearance Drill	Outside Diameter
0	80	1.25	1.60	0.0600
1	72	1.55	1.95	0.0730
2	64	1.90	2.30	0.0860
3	56	2.15	2.65	0.0990
4	48	2.40	2.95	0.1120
5	44	2.70	3.30	0.1250
6	40	2.95	3.60	0.1380
8	36	3.50	4.30	0.1640
10	32	4.10	4.90	0.1900
12	28	4.60	5.60	0.2160
Size Fractions	TPI	Tapping Drill	Clearance Drill	Outside Diameter
$\frac{1}{4}$ in	28	5.50	6.50	0.2500
$\frac{5}{16}$ in	24	6.90	8.10	0.3125
$\frac{3}{8}$ in	24	8.50	9.70	0.3750
$\frac{7}{16}$ in	20	9.90	11.30	0.4375
$\frac{1}{2}$ in	20	11.40	13.00	0.5000
$\frac{9}{16}$ in	18	12.90	14.50	0.5626
$\frac{5}{8}$ in	18	14.50	16.25	0.6250

UNIFIED COARSE

Size Numbers	TPI	Tapping Drill	Clearance Drill	Outside Diameter
1	64	1.5	1.95	0.0730
2	56	1.8	2.30	0.0860
3	48	2.1	2.70	0.0990
4	40	2.3	3.00	0.1120
5	40	2.6	3.30	0.1250
6	32	2.8	3.60	0.1380
8	32	3.5	4.30	0.1640
10	24	3.9	5.00	0.1900
12	24	4.5	5.60	0.2160
Size Fractions	TPI	Tapping Drill	Clearance Drill	Outside Diameter
$\frac{1}{4}$ in	20	5.2	6.50	0.2500
$\frac{5}{16}$ in	18	6.6	8.10	0.3125
$\frac{3}{8}$ in	16	8.0	9.70	0.3750
$\frac{7}{16}$ in	14	9.4	11.30	0.4375
$\frac{1}{2}$ in	13	10.8	13.00	0.500
$\frac{9}{16}$ in	12	12.20	14.50	0.5625
$\frac{5}{8}$ in	11	13.50	16.25	0.6250

Unified Coarse Series of threads (UNC) are frequently called ANC or just U/C. They are American and the outside diameters are in imperials measurements. For the sake of continuity with the other threads in the book, tapping and clearance drills are shown in metric form.

ISO METRIC FINE THREAD SERIES

Outside Diameter	Pitch	Tapping Drill	Clearance Drill
1.70	0.35	1.35	1.80
2.00	0.45	1.55	2.10
2.30	0.40	1.90	2.40
2.60	0.45	2.15	2.70
3.00	0.35	2.65	3.10
3.00	0.60	2.40	3.10
4.00	0.50	3.50	4.10
4.00	0.75	3.20	4.10
5.00	0.50	4.50	5.10
5.00	0.90	4.10	5.10
5.50	0.90	4.60	5.60
6.00	0.75	5.20	6.10
8.00	0.75	7.20	8.10
8.00	1.00	7.00	8.10
9.00	1.00	8.00	9.10
10.00	0.75	9.20	10.20
10.00	1.25	8.80	10.20
12.00	1.00	11.00	12.20
12.00	1.50	10.50	12.20
14.00	1.50	12.50	14.25
16.00	1.00	15.00	16.25
20.00	1.00	19.00	20.25
20.00	2.00	18.00	20.25

There are a number of other threads in the series that have been formulated for special purposes, such as spark plugs.

ISO METRIC COARSE THREADS

Outside Diameter	Pitch	Tapping Drill	Clearance Drill
1.00	0.25	0.75	1.05
1.10	0.25	0.85	1.15
1.20	0.25	0.95	1.25
1.40	0.30	1.10	1.45
1.60	0.35	1.25	1.65
1.80	0.35	1.45	1.85
2.00	0.40	1.60	2.05
2.20	0.45	1.75	2.25
2.50	0.45	2.05	2.60
3.00	0.50	2.50	3.10
3.50	0.60	2.90	3.60
4.00	0.70	3.30	4.10
4.50	0.75	3.70	4.60
5.00	0.80	4.20	5.10
6.00	1.00	5.00	6.10
7.00	1.00	6.00	7.20
8.00	1.25	6.80	8.20
9.00	1.25	7.80	9.20
10.00	1.50	8.50	10.20
11.00	1.50	9.50	11.20
12.00	1.75	10.20	12.20
14.00	2.00	12.00	14.25
16.00	2.00	14.00	16.25

This is the series of threads that is now widely regarded as standard and unless a pitch is specified it is assumed to be the thread referred to.

MODEL ENGINEER (ME) THREADS: TAPPING AND CLEARANCE DRILLS

These threads were devised specially for model engineering purposes. Where pipe fittings, etc. are concerned 100% engagement is desirable. Drill sizes are given in metric. Imperial drills of the nominal thread diameter can also be used for clearance purposes. 26 TPI threads are also known as brass threads.

Size	40 TPI		32 TPI		26 TPI		Clearance	
	100% – 80%		100% – 80%		100% – 80%		100%	102%
$\frac{1}{8}$ in	2.4	2.6					3.2	3.3
$\frac{5}{32}$ in	3.2	3.4	3.0	3.2			4.0	4.1
$\frac{3}{16}$ in	4.0	4.2	3.8	4.0			4.8	4.9
$\frac{7}{32}$ in	4.8	5.0	4.6	4.8			5.6	5.7
$\frac{1}{4}$ in	5.6	5.8	5.4	5.6	5.2	5.4	6.4	6.5
$\frac{9}{32}$ in	6.4	6.5	6.2	6.4	5.9	6.2	7.2	7.3
$\frac{5}{16}$ in	7.2	7.3	7.0	7.3	6.7	7.0	8.0	8.2
$\frac{3}{8}$ in	8.8	8.9	8.6	8.8	8.3	8.6	9.6	9.8
$\frac{7}{16}$ in	10.4	10.5	10.2	10.4	9.9	10.2	11.2	11.4
$\frac{1}{2}$ in	11.9	12.1	11.7	11.9	11.5	11.8	12.8	13.0

BRITISH STANDARD NUMBER AND LETTER DRILLS

The old system of numbered and lettered drills is now virtually obsolete. Many old drawings will still refer to drills in this way and this chart enables accurate conversions to be made.

Gauge	mm	Imp	Gauge	mm	Imp	Gauge	mm	Imp	Letter	mm	Imp
80	0.343	0.0135	55	1.321	0.0520	28	3.569	0.1045	A	5.944	0.2340
79	0.368	0.0145	54	1.397	0.0550	27	3.658	0.1440	B	6.045	0.2380
78	0.406	0.0160	53	1.511	0.0595	26	3.734	0.1470	C	6.147	0.2420
77	0.457	0.0180	52	1.613	0.0635	25	3.797	0.1495	D	6.248	0.2460
76	0.508	0.0200	51	1.702	0.0670	24	3.861	0.1520	E	6.350	0.2500
75	0.533	0.0210	50	1.778	0.0700	23	3.912	0.1540	F	6.528	0.2570
74	0.572	0.0225	49	1.854	0.0730	22	3.988	0.1570	G	6.629	0.2610
73	0.610	0.0240	48	1.930	0.0760	21	4.039	0.1590	H	6.756	0.2660
72	0.635	0.0250	47	1.994	0.0785	20	4.089	0.1610	I	6.909	0.2720
71	0.660	0.0260	46	2.057	0.0810	19	4.216	0.1660	J	7.036	0.2770
70	0.711	0.0280	45	2.083	0.0820	18	4.305	0.1695	K	7.137	0.2810
69	0.742	0.0292	44	2.184	0.0860	17	4.394	0.1730	L	7.366	0.2900
68	0.787	0.0310	43	2.261	0.0890	16	4.496	0.1770	M	7.493	0.2950
67	0.813	0.0320	42	2.375	0.0935	15	4.572	0.1800	N	7.671	0.3020
66	0.838	0.0330	41	2.438	0.0960	14	4.623	0.1820	O	8.026	0.3160
65	0.889	0.0350	40	2.489	0.0980	13	4.700	0.1850	P	8.204	0.3230
66	0.838	0.0330	39	2.527	0.0995	12	4.800	0.1890	Q	8.433	0.3320
65	0.889	0.0350	38	2.578	0.1015	11	4.851	0.1910	R	8.611	0.3390
64	0.914	0.0360	37	2.642	0.1040	10	4.915	0.1935	S	8.839	0.3480
63	0.940	0.0370	36	2.705	0.1065	9	4.978	0.1960	T	9.093	0.3580
62	0.965	0.0380	35	2.794	0.1100	8	5.055	0.1990	U	9.347	0.3680
61	0.991	0.0390	34	2.189	0.1110	7	5.105	0.2010	V	9.576	0.3770
60	1.016	0.0400	33	2.870	0.1130	6	5.182	0.2040	W	9.804	0.3860
59	1.041	0.0410	32	2.946	0.1160	5	5.220	0.2055	X	10.084	0.3970
58	1.067	0.0420	31	3.048	0.1200	4	5.309	0.2090	Y	10.262	0.4040
57	1.092	0.0430	30	3.264	0.1285	3	5.410	0.2310	Z	10.490	0.4130
56	1.181	0.0465	29	3.454	0.1360	2	5.613	0.2210	*	*****	*****
**	****	*****	**	*****	*****	1	5.791	0.2280	*	*****	*****

BRITISH ASSOCIATION THREADS (BA)

Size (Number)	Outside Dia. Inch	Outside Dia. mm	Threads Per Inch	Tapping Drill mm	Clearance Drill mm
0	0.2362	6.0	25.38	5.10	6.00
1	0.1850	5.3	28.25	4.50	5.40
2	0.1850	4.7	31.35	4.00	4.80
3	0.1614	4.1	34.84	3.45	4.20
4	0.1417	3.6	38.46	3.00	3.70
5	0.1260	3.2	43.10	2.65	3.30
6	0.1102	2.8	47.85	2.30	2.85
7	0.0984	2.5	52.91	2.05	2.55
8	0.0866	2.2	59.17	1.80	2.25
9	0.0748	1.9	64.94	1.55	1.95
10	0.0669	1.7	72.46	1.40	1.80
11	0.0591	1.5	81.97	1.20	1.50
12	0.0511	1.3	90.91	1.05	1.30
13	0.0470	1.2	102.04	0.90	1.20
14	0.0390	1.0	109.89	0.72	1.00
15	0.0350	0.9	120.48	0.65	0.65
16	0.0310	0.8	133.33	0.56	0.80

BRITISH STANDARD FINE (BSF)

Size	Threads Per Inch	Tapping Drill	Clearance Drill
$\frac{1}{8}$ in	48	2.9	3.3
$\frac{3}{16}$ in	32	4.0	4.8
$\frac{1}{4}$ in	26	5.30	6.40
$\frac{9}{32}$ in	26	6.10	7.20
$\frac{5}{16}$ in	22	6.80	8.00
$\frac{3}{8}$ in	20	8.30	9.60
$\frac{7}{16}$ in	18	9.70	11.20
$\frac{1}{2}$ in	16	11.10	12.70
$\frac{5}{8}$ in	14	14.00	16.00
$\frac{11}{16}$ in	14	15.50	17.50
$\frac{3}{4}$ in	12	16.75	19.25
$\frac{7}{8}$ in	11	19.75	22.25
1 in	10	22.75	25.50

Appendix II
Chords

To divide a circle into segments take the length of the chord relevant to the number required and multiply it by the diameter of the circle.

No. of Spaces	Chord length	No. of Spaces	Chord Length	No. of Spaces	Chord Length
3	0.8660	23	0.1362	43	0.0730
4	0.7071	24	0.1305	44	0.0713
5	0.5878	25	0.1253	45	0.0698
6	0.5000	26	0.1205	46	0.0682
7	0.4339	27	0.1161	47	0.0668
8	0.3827	28	0.1120	48	0.0654
9	0.3420	29	0.1081	49	0.0641
10	0.3090	30	0.1045	50	0.0628
11	0.2817	31	0.1012	51	0.0616
12	0.2588	32	0.0980	52	0.0604
13	0.2393	33	0.0951	53	0.0592
14	0.2225	34	0.0923	54	0.0581
15	0.2079	35	0.0896	55	0.0571
16	0.1951	36	0.0872	56	0.0561
17	0.1838	37	0.0848	57	0.0551
18	0.1736	38	0.0826	58	0.0541
19	0.1646	39	0.0805	59	0.0532
20	0.1564	40	0.0785	60	0.0523
21	0.1490	41	0.0765	61	0.0515
22	0.1423	42	0.0747	62	0.0507

CHORDS

No. of Spaces	Chord length	No. of Spaces	Chord Length	No. of Spaces	Chord Length
63	0.0499	76	0.0413	89	0.0353
64	0.0491	77	0.0408	90	0.0349
65	0.0483	78	0.0403	91	0.0345
66	0.0476	79	0.0398	92	0.0341
67	0.0469	80	0.0393	93	0.0338
68	0.0462	81	0.0388	94	0.0334
69	0.0455	82	0.0383	95	0.0331
70	0.0449	83	0.0378	96	0.0327
71	0.0442	84	0.0374	97	0.0324
72	0.0436	85	0.0370	98	0.0321
73	0.0430	86	0.0365	99	0.0317
74	0.0424	87	0.0361	100	0.0314
75	0.0419	88	0.0357	–	–

Index

INDEX

176